Current Challenges in Migration Policy and Law

Current Challenges in Migration Policy and Law

Edited by

Emília Lana de Freitas Castro and
Sergio Maia Tavares Marques

TRANSNATIONAL PRESS LONDON

2020

Current Challenges in Migration Policy and Law

Edited by

Emília Lana de Freitas Castro and Sergio Maia Tavares Marques

Copyright © 2020 Transnational Press London

First Published in 2020 by TRANSNATIONAL PRESS LONDON in the United Kingdom, 12 Ridgeway Gardens, London, N6 5XR, UK.
www.tplondon.com

Transnational Press London® and the logo and its affiliated brands are registered trademarks.

Requests for permission to reproduce material from this work should be sent to: sales@tplondon.com

Paperback
ISBN: 978-1-910781-77-7

Cover Design: Gizem Çakır
Cover Photo: 19.12.2017, Serbia, Belgrad Refugees people on the balkan route by Janossy Gergely/Shutterstock.com

www.tplondon.com

CONTENTS

ABOUT THE EDITORS AND CONTRIBUTORS

Emília Lana de Freitas Castro defended her PhD at Universität Hamburg in 2019. Her thesis, entitled "The Free Movement of Voluntary Immigrants and their Freedom of Settlement in a Comparative Perspective: The Legal Frameworks of Migration in Brazil and the MERCOSUL and the Legal Frameworks in Germany and the EU as a Parameter of Comparison" has been given the grade magna cum laude. During her PhD, she held a scholarship from CAPES (Coordenadoria de Aperfeiçoamento de Pessoal de Nível Superior), an entity of the Brazilian Ministry of Culture. She holds a Bachelor of Laws and a Master in International Law from the Universidade do Estado do Rio de Janeiro (UERJ). She is a Brazilian qualified lawyer and worked as an Assistant Lecturer for Private International Law at UERJ (2013 and 2014) and as a lecturer for Brazilian Private International Law at Universität Hamburg (2017 and 2018).

Sergio Maia Tavares Marques is a PhD candidate at the Catholic University of Portugal. He holds a masters degree in EU Law from the University of Minho (2017), where he is a researcher at the Centre of Studies in EU Law (CEDU), lecturer for EU Law and managing editor of UNIO – EU Law Journal. For his master thesis, entitled "The public reason of the Union based on the rule of law: from lawfulness to social democratisation" he was awarded the Jacques Delors Prize in 2018. He is a member of ICON.S Portugal. Sergio is a qualified lawyer and currently works as référendaire at the Constitutional Court of Portugal.

Anita C. Butera received her PhD in Sociology with a specialization in Racial and Ethnic Conflict within the Postindustrial Economy from The American University, Washington DC (USA) and her J.D. from SUNY-Buffalo School of Law (USA) with a focus on International Law and Human Rights. An active member of the New York Bar, she is also admitted to practice in Federal Court, Western and Northern District of New York as well as the 9th Circuit. Prior of joining Canisius College, she taught at College of Law, Prince Mohammed bin Fahad University, in Al-Khobar (KSA) and Marist College, in Poughkeepsie NY (USA). Dr Butera has conducted research in the field of race-ethnic conflict and economic restructuring, human rights, Sharia Law, Philosophy of Law as well as Bankruptcy Reform. As a lawyer, she has represented undocumented migrant workers and victims of human trafficking.

Secil E. Ertorer received her PhD in Sociology with a specialization in

Migration and Ethnic Relations from The University of Western Ontario, Canada. She taught at the University of Western Ontario, King's University College, and York University before joining Canisius College in 2017. Dr. Ertorer's research interests are in the areas of international migration, refugee studies, integration, and identity. She has conducted fieldwork in England, Canada, and Turkey, interviewing Kurdish, Turkish, Karen, Burmese, and Syrian refugees and representatives of humanitarian agencies, focusing on settlement and integration experiences as well as re-formation of identities in the process of migration.

Sureyya Sonmez Efe currently works as a Lecturer in Politics and International Relations at the University of Lincoln. She studied European Studies (BA Hons) at The Open University, followed by Globalising Justice: Human Rights, Crime and Social Justice (PG) at University of Lincoln, and completed her PhD in Political Science at Leeds Beckett University in 2017. Sureyya's research is on 'the rights of migrant workers in contemporary Turkey' which takes an interdisciplinary approach to the analysis of legal status and rights of migrant workers at national and international levels. Through developing the theory of 'porous values', this research is important in terms of pushing the boundaries of politics of migration designed under states' jurisdiction by including the 'rights perspective' into the process of policy-making. Sureyya's current research looks into the integration process of migrants and minorities into the host communities which focuses on states' integration policies such as 'cohesion programmes in Europe'.

Melina Duarte is an internationally educated political philosopher, specialised in migration scholarship. She is currently a post-doctoral researcher affiliated to the Department of Philosophy, Faculty of Humanities and Social Sciences, UiT The Arctic University of Norway. Her research centers on immigration and borders, national and democratic citizenship, and human rights and international law. She is particularly preoccupied with disclosing new ways in which the mobility of persons across borders could be handled while respecting both human rights and state sovereignty. Duarte's work has been published in Portuguese, French, English, German and Norwegian. Contact: melina.duarte@uit.no

Giulia Manccini Pinheiro is an international lawyer with bachelor's in law from the Federal University of Santa Catarina, Brazil and Master's in International Law from the Graduate Institute of International and Development Studies, Switzerland. Moreover, she is a researcher from the South America Network on Environmental Migration (RESAMA). Giulia has been researching on the interactions of human mobility, climate change, disaster and human-rights law since 2014 and has held a PIBIC/CNPq research fellowship.

Carsten Schäfer is an assistant professor at the Institute of East Asian Studies (department for Chinese Studies) at the University of Cologne, Germany. Between 2011 and 2015 he worked at the Department of East Asian

Studies/Sinology, University of Vienna, Austria. He studied in Freiburg/Br. (Germany), Shanghai (China), and Vienna and received his PhD in 2018. His research interests include Chinese migration, overseas Chinese politics, Greater China studies, and the historiography of the People's Republic of China. He is currently working on projects on China's diaspora policies and the image of Xi Jinping in Chinese propaganda. In his leisure time, he translates modern Chinese literature into German.

Annalisa Geraci is a PhD student at the University of Teramo (Italy). She attends the PhD in "International Perspectives in Corporate Governance and Public Administration" with a research project entitled: "EU migration policies at the crossroads of humanitarian disasters and solidarity". She collaborates with the chairs of Public Law, International Law and European Law at the Faculty of Political Science. Her publications include "Unaccompanied minors in international, European and Italian law. Current weaknesses and future prospects", La Comunità Internazionale, 4/2017; "There is not enough union in this Union". Principio di solidarietà e "Sistema di Dublino" alla prova del più imponente esodo di profughi dal secondo dopoguerra, www.federalismi.it, 2016.

Roila Mavrouli is a lawyer and a PhD candidate at the University of Luxembourg in cotutelle with the University of Paris Nanterre. Roila holds a Bachelor's degree in Law of the Aristotle University of Thessaloniki, a Master's degree in International and European public law of the University Jean Moulin Lyon 3 and a Master's Degree in Political Philosophy of the University Paris 7 Diderot. She has worked as a lawyer in Athens and as a legal counsel focusing on migration law and fundamental rights in Paris and in Luxembourg. During the last years, she has been teaching Constitutional law at the University Paris 13 and European law at the University of Luxembourg. She has been an active volunteer with various asylum law associations and she has participated in many conferences and workshops. Her research focuses on legal theory and jurisprudence from the perspective of a realistic critical approach to the traditional legal concepts and the validity of the norms.

INTRODUCTION

Emília Lana de Freitas Castro and Sergio Maia Tavares Marques

This book brings together a selection of the contributions presented (and later revised and edited) at The Migration Conference (TMC) 2018, held from the 26th to the 28th of June in Lisbon and hosted by Lisbon School of Economics & Management (ISEG - *Instituto Superior de Economia e Gestão*) and by The Institute of Geography and Spatial Planning (IGOT – *Instituto de Geografia e Ordenamento do Território*), both of them belonging to the University of Lisbon. Chaired by Ibrahim Sirkeci, João Peixoto and Maria Lucinda Fonseca, the conference was organised in thematic streams of about 140 parallel sessions and three plenary sessions, along with two developmental workshops, one photography exhibition, and four short movie screenings over the three days. Over 500 participants from about 60 countries attended TMC 2018. Just as it happened in the previous years, the 2018 edition of TMC was a forum for discussions where experts, young researches and students, practitioners and policymakers working in the field of migration joined the debate and exchanged their knowledge and experiences.

This book emerges from those fruitful discussions as a collection of some of the matters presented, whose authors have virtuously stood out. Just as the previous books that arose from other TMC editions, *Current Challenges in Migration Policy and Law* gives the opportunity not only to experienced professors and researches but especially to young scholars to divulge their studies and present their experiences in the various research fields migration can be discussed, rethought and further developed. We are thankful to Transnational Press London as it believed in our aspirations as editors and it stimulated us to be protagonists in the process of editing and building up this book the way we believed it would contribute to the current discussions on migration. As scholars and young researchers, we are delighted by this opportunity created by Professor Sirkeci.

Differently from the other chapters of the present book, Chapter 1, written by Anita Butera and Secil Ertorer, is a paper that was presented in The Migration Conference 2019, which was hosted in June by the University of Bari, in Italy. The editors decided to add this paper from the 2019 Conference to the present book due to its extreme importance by connecting the capitalist system to the perception native workers attribute to immigrant workers and by linking migrant's social conditions and economy. In Chapter 1, named as *Restrictive asylum policies and reflections in the labour market: the cases of Italy and Turkey*, the abovementioned authors analyse within the context of the capitalist market how the asylum and immigration law of the states benefit capitalist economies by legally creating a vulnerable and precarious working class, consisting of refugees, asylum seekers, and undocumented migrants. The authors do a comparative migration policy analysis between Italy and Turkey, and they argue that the immigration legal framework socially constructs refugees as others who have no rights to work or stay and that this condition fosters a general perception against immigrants as the native workers attribute to them a decline in economic opportunities.

In a similar vein, Sureyya Sonmez Efe states in Chapter 2 that international labour migration is arguably one of the most sensitive topics of politics of migration. She asks: *How far do moral values shape the legal terminology used in international conventions concerning migrant workers?* State's reluctance in providing a rights-based approach to labour migration causes a restrictive approach to admissions, residence and rights of migrant workers. The author believes that there is a lack of a unified moral approach to international labour migration once International Law gives the states the possibility to design their migration policies. In this sense, Sureyya Sonmez Efe understands that socially constructed moral values gravely affect the legal terminology adopted by international conventions on labour migration which are crucial for the recognition of the status and protection of migrant worker´s rights.

Chapters 3 and 4 ponder on the interplay between climate change and migration and which we consider being one of the most relevant topics on migration studies for the next years. In Chapter 3, written by Melina Duarte, it is affirmed that residents of areas that turned uninhabitable and were therefore forced to relocate in the wake of climate changes justify a moral extension of human rights protection. It is for this reason that Duarte´s paper titled *A human right to relocate: the case for climate migrants* justifies an expansion of human rights by arguing that a right to relocate for climate migrants carries enough moral weight to be turned into a human right and therefore be included in human rights law. Referring to Chapter 4, named *Climate change migration as an adaptation strategy: the adaptation approach theory and the Paris Agreement*, Giulia Manccini Pinheiro investigates the adaptation approach theory and scrutinises whether or not the Paris Agreement addresses the challenges climate change poses. Also, Pinheiro adds to her analysis of how national commitments have incorporated the adaptation approach theory.

Chapter 5, written by Carsten Schäfer, examines China's diaspora policies using the case of Chinese immigrants in Austria. In his paper *Whose diaspora? Rethinking diaspora politics: China's overseas Chinese engagement in transnational spaces,* Schäfer goes beyond official actions and proposes a theoretical reconceptualization of diaspora engagement politics. One of Schäfer's main research question is how China's diaspora politics are exploited and re-shaped by Chinese overseas and, in order to explore this topic, he covers power relations encompassing multiple actors at both national and transnational levels.

Annalisa Geraci, in Chapter 6, touches upon the specific issue of the EU-Turkey Statement for dealing with the so-called "refugee crisis", especially when it comes to the "1:1 scheme" actions. In her paper entitled *"Out of sight, out of mind". Managing migration flows with Turkey as a "safe third country"*, Geraci ascertains the potential application of the concept of "safe third country" to Turkey by doing a formal and substantive analysis of Turkey´s asylum system. The author also emphasizes and proves how the EU's externalization of its migration policy leads to a degradation of refugee protection standards.

Lastly, in Chapter 7, Roila Mavrouli with her text *"Soft law, effectiveness of fundamental rights and migration: how effective are migrants´ fundamental rights in an era of European governance?"* examines the increment of procedural rationality in the field of fundamental rights issues concerning migration from non-EU countries. The author inquiries the possibility to transform the valorisation of procedural rationality to essential rationality and sustains that this practice has shaped the systematization of procedures related to detention and return of immigrants within the EU. Mavrouli cites the concept of procedural rationality as the one being capable of establishing soft law as the fastest and most flexible solution to the migration challenge. Her question, thus, is if the clash of democracy and bureaucracy could mean the ineffectiveness of fundamental rights through soft law.

We encourage every migration researcher, professor, and scholar to use this collective book shaped by the contributions of authors from such different backgrounds as an instrument for his/her daily work. We hope the discussions brought by this book can enrich people's academic work and can inspire scholars to the new ways of thinking about the movement of people around the globe.

CHAPTER 1

RESTRICTIVE ASYLUM POLICIES AND REFLECTIONS IN THE LABOUR MARKET: THE CASES OF ITALY AND TURKEY

Anita C. Butera and Secil Ertorer

Introduction

The term globalization has been a main topic of political and academic debate since late 1980s. Broadly speaking, globalization refers to free movement of goods, service and people in an integrated manner; referred as coming all countries together. One of the main characteristics of globalization is the increase in migratory flows of people as a result of political, economic, or environmental causes as well as easier access to information, means of travel and communication.

Following the political turbulences such as the collapse of socialist regimes in Eastern Europe and more recently the civil war in Syria, there has been a dramatic increase in the migration flows in Europe. In this new era, some countries such as Italy and Turkey, that are traditionally known as the senders of emigrants to Europe and North America, have emerged as receivers of high volume of immigrants and refugees. This paper argues that the shift in international migration patterns has redefined the dynamics of the labour market in receiving societies. Focusing on the amplified refugee flows in the region of Europe, this paper explores the link between migration and the dramatic decline of protected labour, which is the type of employment that is regulated and protected by the labour law. An analysis of immigration and asylum laws of Italy and Turkey reveals that the law facilitates and legitimizes a dual labour market by classifying labourers in the market as legal or illegal persons and defining their ability and limitations to enter the labour market. In both countries, the legal framework prompts a further segmentation of the already divided dual-labour markets.

The dual labour market consists of primary and secondary labour markets (Pirore, 1979), the former identified by protected conditions for the qualified labourer and the further by precarity. This paper discusses that following the influx of asylum seekers and refugees, the secondary labour market also gets divided into two segments. The traditional segment continues to be occupied by legal labourer who are disadvantaged due to their qualifications or social identity. The new lower segment is occupied by vulnerable groups such as refugees and others who are not recognised as legal persons by the law thus afraid to report poor conditions or abuse to authorities. The emergency of this split in the secondary labour market has redefined labour relations with legal labourer being replaced by the workers who are not recognised as legal labourers by the law, whenever it is possible, consequently narrowing the protected class and generating antagonism against undocumented workers who are threatening secure positions.

The current study aims to contribute to the evolving literature on refugee experiences in receiving societies in general and labour market experiences of refugees in particular by providing a policy analysis and linking it to the theories of homologue of commodity (Pashukanis,1924), dual-labour market (Pirore, 1979), and reserve army of labour (Marx, 1867).

Immigrants and refugees: the legal construction of labour exploitation

According to the neoclassical theory, free labour market is a key element of economic prosperity. In a free market, employers and employees are free agents endowed with equal rights who decide and specify mutual rights and obligations in a labour contract (Vercherand, 2014). This is an expression of the ideology of the superior morality of the capitalist mode of production since it embodies "freedom" and "formal equality" of both employers and employees. In other words, the law, through the labour contract, guarantees the morality of capitalist labour relations. However, in spite of this ideology of "freedom" and "formal equality", capitalism has historically developed and prospered through the exploitation of labour. To name a few examples, capitalist economies flourished through the exploitation of slave labour in the Americas between the 17th and 19th centuries, mineworkers in South Africa in the 20th and 21st centuries, foreign workers in Europe after World War II, and trafficked, undocumented migrants and refugees in Europe, Asia, and North America in the late 20th and 21st centuries (Cohen, 1987; Castles, De Hass, Miller, 2014). The question, therefore, is how this ideology of "freedom" and "formal equality" has fared to foster and justify the exploitation of labour. The answer lays in the ways labour and labour relations are defined by the law.

As argued by Pashukanis, the legal form is dialectically determined by the commodity form (Pashukanis, 1924). To be exchanged in the market, commodities must be turned into juridical objects and to enter the market individuals must be turned into legal subjects. This turns people into "free" and formally equal "legal persons"[1] asserting their legally defined rights over legally

---

[1] This is the legal fiction of Personhood or the legal status of being a person having the right to legally act on his/her behalf. A legal person can also be a non-person such as in the case of a Corporation.

defined "things." This makes the legal form a homologue of the commodity[2] for the reason that, within the capitalist market, the commodity is defined by the law. For example, in a capitalist market, a house is sold through the exchange of a document, the deed, that legally defines the house and the house is transferred from the seller to the buyer by another legal document, the contract. In a similar vein, in a capitalist economy, labour is a commodity that must acquire a legal form to be sold in the market. However, the legal form of labour varies depending on who is the seller and who is the labourer or performer of the labour[3] as well as how the law defines labour as a commodity.

Within the capitalist market, labour is free or unfree depending on who is the "legal person" entitled to sell labour as a commodity. For instance, in slavery, the labourer, who is the slave, is unfree to sell his/her labour since s/he is legally considered as chattel property, hence does not have a legal personality. The owner of the slave can enter the labour market to sell the slave's labour. Similarly, within the relation of indentured servitude, the labourer is the servant or indentured employee and s/he cannot sell his/her labour to a third party for the duration of the indenture contract as indentured employer has the exclusive right to use his/her labour. The capitalist system has the ability to regulate the extreme form of labour exploitation by keeping the labour relationship outside of the labour law. This way, the ideology of superior morality of capitalist labour relations is not debated since the law defines unfree labourers not as workers/legal subjects who enter in an equal and free relationship in the market, but as property/legal objects.

For free labour, the law defines and regulates labour as a commodity along a continuum ranging from protected to precarious. In a labour contract, there are varying degrees of freedom of the parties to negotiate the terms. In the form of protected labour, which is usually achieved by collective bargaining or government regulations, the negotiation powers of the buyer and seller are limited by the state and work conditions are partially defined by the state. Protected conditions grant the worker basic rights not only in terms of conditions of employment but also in terms of decreased dependence on wages through a safety net. For example, unemployment benefits and paid family leave are all legal rights that decrease the dependence of the worker on wages. Precarious labour conditions, instead, are those labour relations which are only marginally (if at all) regulated by the state. Precarious labour is

defined by uncertainty as to the duration of employment, multiple possible employers or a disguised or ambiguous employment relationship, a lack of access to social protection and benefits usually associated with employment, low pay, and substantial legal and practical obstacles to joining a trade union and bargaining collectively (ILO, 2011, p.5).

---

[2] It asserts that commodities exchanged in the market are defined through the legal form they assu Pashukanis me in the market. As a result, they are the homologue of each other's because the legal form is the expression of the material form and they exist in a dialectical relation with each other.
[3] This paper defines the performer of the labour as labourer. The labourer is not always the one who sells his/her labour in the market.

Since precarious labour is associated with marginal government protection, it increases the dependence of the worker on the labour market. In post-industrial economies, as a result of legal reforms weakening government regulations of labour relations and the weakening of the bargain powers of workers due to the decline of unionization, precarious labour relations have emerged as the most common form of labour traded in the market. As a result, within the current phase of globalization, workers, lacking the protection of the government, are highly dependent on the labour market.

This paper asserts that the analysis of refugee labour is essential in understanding the extension of precarious labour segment in the labour market without prompting a crisis of legitimacy of capital accumulation. Building on the theoretical assumption that the law defines and legitimizes exploitation of labour, this paper argues that the law legitimizes the exploitation of refugee labour through limiting their right to sell their own labour and participate in the free market as equals.

The 1951 UN Convention and Protocol of Refugees define an 'asylum seeker' as a person who leaves his/her home country for seeking asylum in another as a political refugee and a political 'refugee' as someone having

well-founded fear of being persecuted for reasons of race, religion, nationality, membership of a particular social group or political opinion, is out-side the country of his nationality and is unable or, owing to such fear, is unwilling to avail himself of the protection of that country; or who, not having a nationality and being outside the country of his former habitual residence as a result of such events, is unable or, owing to such fear, is unwilling to return to it (Art. 1, Refugees Convention 1951).

While this definition encompasses both citizens and stateless individuals, it restricts the status of refugees to those who have a "well-founded fear" of prosecution due to their "race, religion, nationality, membership to a social group or political opinion." This definition identifies refugees as political and the states may not grant this status to individuals owing to political reasons. Since it is less political, a temporary 'humanitarian relief' status is seen as an alternative to refugee status. For example, an adulterous who is afraid of having to face the death penalty upon his/her return to Saudi Arabia or Iran is unlikely to be granted the status of refugee but may be granted temporary status on humanitarian grounds. This gives the national law system the ability to regulate legal participation of asylum seekers and refugees into the social life and the labour market in the receiving country by creating several legal classifications that come with varying rights.

By granting the asylum seeker a temporary (humanitarian protection) or permanent status (as a refugee) or by denying a status and initiating deportation procedures, the law defines the type of status under which the asylum seeker will enter the labour market, thus, the level of precarity of his/her labour. When the law defines a labourer as "temporary", "rightless" or "undocumented," it denies his/her power of contractual negotiation in the labour market. As a result, the labourer ends up either by not participating in the labour market at all, or selling labour as a commodity in the illegal economy and accepting forced conditions and terms. Thus, the form of refugees' participation into the labour market is defined by the legal framework of the country; in particular, by its asylum and migration law. Moreover, since the status of asylum applicants are defined and regulated by the asylum and migration law, not the labour law, the state takes no responsibility of precarity or exploitation, maintaining the ideology of moral superiority of capitalist labour relations. At the same time, that fosters nationalistic and populist rhetoric because the decline of protected labour, which is in fact independent of the existence of immigrant labour in the economy, is seen not as a consequence of the process of capital accumulation and a form of labour exploitation, but as a consequence of unprecedented influx of immigration. To further apprehend the role of refugee labour in maintaining the ideology of moral superiority of capitalist labour relations and justification of labour exploitation, the concept of formal equality must be analyzed.

Formal equality is a well-established principle of the western legal tradition (Harold, 1983). This principle refers to the belief that the law is impartial and equally applies to the sides in a social relationship. However, formal equality does not alter the power relationship between the seller and the buyer of labour (Smith, 2000). It is, therefore, a powerful tool to legitimize exploitation and maintain the ideology of moral superiority of capitalist labour relations. The idea that 'we are all equal under the law' makes humans to believe that they relate to each other as equals. In other words, formal equality is perceived as political equality and economic inequality is seen as an individual problem, not a defining feature of capitalism. The moral superiority of capitalist labour relations is further reinforced by the ability of the legal system to regulate only some forms of labour under labour law. For example, the work performed by homemakers is not regulated by labour law. Indeed, a key difference between free and unfree labour is whether the seller of labour is the labourer and whether the labour transaction is regulated by the labour law.

Free labour is regulated by labour law because the seller is the labourer and both the seller and buyer are defined by the law as free agents endowed with equal rights. On the contrary, unfree labour is not regulated by labour law because the labourer is not legally able to sell his/her labour and is not entitled to equal right as the buyer. The ability of the law to bring some forms of labour outside of the labour law gives legitimacy to labour exploitation as labourers are not seen as workers. For instance, the exploitation of prisoner labour is morally justified by perceiving them as prisoners, not workers. Similarly, the exploitation of refugee labour is morally justified because they are perceived not as workers, but as refugees. This can be seen as the process of socio-legal construction of refugees as 'others': Since refugees are not one of 'us' or legally equal to us, their struggle is their own and their exploitation is not a relevant element of the capitalist labour market (Nunez, 2013). This creates a condition of high exploitability without questioning the morality of capitalist labour relations. Within post-industrial economies, this socio-legal construction of the 'other' has played a key role in the significant expansion of precarious labour and altered the composition of the "reserve of army labour" (Marx, 1867).

The "reserve army of labour" is the segment of the labour force to be held in reserve and used when the need arises at times of labour shortage or increased class-consciousness (Marx, 1867). Marx divides the reserve army of labour into three categories: floating, latent, and stagnant. The floating part consists of workers working on short cyclical periods defined by industrial production cycle. The latent part is formed by flows of labour moving from one area to another as motivated by urbanization and industrialization. Finally, the stagnant part includes those employed under extremely irregular and highly exploited conditions (Marx, 1867; Grover and Piggott, 2005). Within the current phase of globalization, refugees are the largest component of both latent and stagnant reserve army of labour. However, their utilization as the reserve army of labour creates ethnic antagonism (Bonacich, 1972) between refugees and nationals who are traditional holders of the positions placed by refugees. Therefore, the 'otherization' of asylum seekers and refugees through the socio-legal processes contributes to the increase in precarious labour and ethnic tensions in post-industrial societies.

Advanced economies demand both highly skilled workers and lower-skilled manual workers which brings about a division into primary and secondary labour markets (Pirore, 1979). This division creates a segmented labour market in which the workers in the primary market are not selected only by the criteria of human capital, but also by ethnicity, race, gender, and legal status in the country. Workers who are disadvantaged by their gender or racial identity or their legal status in the country end up in the secondary sector even if they have human capital required for the primary sector jobs. Immigrants with no legal status (undocumented, asylum seekers, temporarily protected, etc.) consist the most vulnerable and docile segment in the labour force, with having no rights and facing the threat of deportation. By denying them legal status and basic rights, immigration policies serve to "facilitate and legitimize exploitation of migrants in the labour market" (Castles et. al., 2009, p.36).

In sum, refugee labour plays a crucial role in the increase of labour precarity without prompting a legitimacy crisis of capitalism in post-industrial societies. This is a consequence of socio-legal otherization of refugees and utilization of refugees to redefine increasing class inequalities along nationalistic lines. Therefore, the status and experiences of refugees must be analyzed within the context of capitalist market and in relation to the law defining their position as well as legitimizing their exploitation.

Methodology

A key theoretical assumption of this study is that the law defines the exploitation of labour by designating the legal status of the labourer and the conditions under which his/her labour can be sold on the market. In the case of refugees, it is important to understand how the legal status and rights of refugees defines the exploitation of their labour. In order to understand how migration and refugee laws define the exploitability of refugee labour, this paper incorporates a comparative migration policy analysis of the countries Italy and Turkey. The analysis of migration and asylum policies provides understanding of the legal framework within which exploitation of refugee labour take place. Italy and Turkey are selected as case countries due to their similar geographical position at the crossroads of Asia, Africa, and the European Union (EU). Both countries are considered gateways to Europe being simultaneously sending, destination, and transit countries of post 1989 immigration. Moreover, both countries have been regarded as major emigration countries that serve as labour reserve for industrialized western countries, especially during the reconstruction of Europe after the World War II (Sirkeci and Push, 2016; Del Boca and Venturini, 2003). However, following the mass inflows of refugees, their roles have changed from sending to receiving countries and they have come to share similar concerns of the traditional receiving countries while playing a key role in shaping immigration flows to Europe, thus being under pressure by the EU to control their borders. Neither of the countries were prepared to handle the significant immigrant and refugee inflows nor able to regulate immigration. Both countries adopted policies that systematically deny basic rights to refugees and offer poverty-level social assistance to asylum seekers and irregular migrants that increase refugees' dependence on the labour market and the precarity of their labour. Therefore, a very important step is to analyze the historical evolution of immigration policies and law in both countries as well as their relation to the labour market.

From State Building to Emergency Management: The History of Migration Law and Policy in Italy and Turkey

The analysis of immigration law is essential for understanding the experiences of precarity in a labour market. A defining role of immigration law is not only to regulate entry to and exit from a country, but also to regulate the labour force in the receiving country in a way to meet the needs and maximize revenues of the economy. For instance, in Europe after the World War II, the labour shortages prompted guest-worker programs such as the German *Gastarbeiterprogramm*. Indeed, the development of immigration law reflects the economic needs of the economy of the receiving country, including the ability of national capital to control the cost of labour. Within the post-industrial economies, migrant labour has a key role in redefining labour relations. Especially in the countries with strong legislation that protects national labour, immigrant labour has been central in promoting precarious forms of labour in specific lower level jobs while reserving some sectors, such as public service or public education, for protected citizen labour. This has been done by fostering the emergency of a split labour market organized along immigration status.

Italy and Turkey are two historical centers of emigration. Until the 1980s, immigration laws were non-existent in Italy and build upon the ideals of nation building in the case of Turkey. In both countries, the situation started to change in late 1970s and early 1980s as a result of large influx of refugees due to Khomeini's Revolutions in Iran and the collapse of socialist regimes in Eastern Europe. Indeed, their geographical position, being at the crossroads between Africa, Europe, and Asia, made them the ports of entry or preferred destination for emigrants. Both Italy and Turkey were forced to modify their immigration and asylum laws to manage the shift from sender to receiver poles of migration. The new legislations regulating asylum seekers also facilitated the precarious conditions within the labour market. Moreover, they fostered a change in the dynamics of the existing dual labour market, with asylum seekers and refugees taking the most precarious positions. This section will outline the historical evolution of migration and asylum laws in Italy and Turkey to better understand the link between the legal framework and labour market relations.

Italy

The Kingdom of Italy was proclaimed on March 17, 1861. Following the annexation of Rome on September 20, 1870 and the speeding up of the industrialization of the Northern regions (Gramsci, 2005), Italy became one of the largest international poles of migration.[4] Contrary to Turkey where citizenship and immigration law fostered the emergency of a national identity based on ethnic and religious identity, Italian citizenship law was solely based on *Jus Sanguine* along patrilineal lines. This reflected the political choice of creating a new national identity based on a *shared Italian identity* mostly based on *language* (Donati, 2013). Moreover, even after Italy had become one of the major poles of international emigration, it did not have a comprehensive immigration law and the only law regulating foreigners within Italian borders was a public security law of 1931 which required foreigners living in Italy to declare their presence to the authorities (Royal Decree No. 773 of 1931). The situation started to change in the late 1970s when the first waves of immigrants started to arrive in Italy in the midle-1970s mostly from the Philippines (IOM, 2010); and, secondly from Iran following the Khomeini's revolution and the Iran-Iraq war (Miggiano, 2015).

The first immigration law, *Legge Foschi*, was passed in 1986. The purpose of this law was to regulate economic immigration by, on one hand, creating a situation of equality between Italian and foreign workers and, on the other, regulating economic employment by establishing a complex system to assess the labour needs of the Italian market. The problem of this law is that it ignored the uniqueness of the Italian labour market, in particular the reality of the *economia sommersa* (underground economy) which employs workers outside of

---

[4] It is estimated that between 1880 and 1976 over 25 million of Italians left Italy with approximately 13 million permanently relocating in the Americas and other European countries such as Germany and France (Ben-Ghiat and Malia Hom, 2016)

nationally negotiated union contracts; the so-called *lavoro in nero*. This includes activities that evade government's control (and taxation) such as street vendors, domestic work, rural daily workers, tailoring, tutoring and so on (Einaudi, 2007). Moreover, the law ignored the fact that an increasing percentage of immigrants were self-employed as street vendors and that most of the hiring in the *economia sommersa* as well as domestic and rural sectors took place on an individual and temporary base (Einaudi, 2007, p. 130). Essentially, the law lacked an understanding of the reality of Italian labour relations and made no efforts to integrate immigrants into Italian labour market or society. The major effect of the law was to consolidate the shift in the composition of the *lavoro in nero*, increasingly occupied by immigrants, and contributed to the creation of a dual labour market along immigration status.

Interestingly, the *Legge Foschi* did not address the status of refugees that continued to be regulated by the 1951 Geneva Convention. According to this Convention, a refugee is someone who is outside of her/his country of origins and unable to return to that country due to a well-founded fear of prosecution.[5] Moreover, the status of refugee is granted to those individuals fleeing their country because of events occurring in Europe or elsewhere before January of 1951. This definition, de facto limited the status of refugees to individuals displaced by the World War II and at the dawn of the Cold War. Being one of the few European countries that grants aliens a constitutional right to apply for asylum, Italian law extends asylum protection also to family members as well as allows foreign citizens who may not qualify for asylum but would face a serious risk to suffer harm to apply for *subsidiary protection*.[6]

A turning point in the Italian immigration debate was the brutal killing of Jerry Masslo, a South African native who was denied refugee status due to non-European citizenship, on August 25, 1989. The public outrage over his death brought public attention to the living conditions of refugees and the increasing racism against *extra-comunitari* (non-European Union immigrants). This event was a defining factor in the passage of the *Legge Martelli* in 1990. A main innovation of this law was the removal of the limitation for asylum seekers established by the 1951 Refugees Convention Art. 1B, allowing everyone to apply for refugee status. While the main purpose of the law was to regularize immigration, it also opened the gate to the Dublin Convention in 1992 which establishes that the country where the asylum application is first filed is responsible for accepting or rejection the application and the seeker cannot refile the application in a different country.[7] Moreover, for the first time, the law introduced immigration quotas and reformed deportation procedures.

The law created two different procedures for deportation. The first is 'administrative deportation' and is applied in the cases of irregularities of entry

---

[5] Refugee Convention, Art. 1A(2); 1B(1)(a)(b)
[6] This is similar to withholding from deportation in US law and extend asylum outside of the political limitation of the 1951 Geneva Convention.
[7] Dublin Regulations, 2013

or stay. This is administered by the local authority, through the office of the *Prefettura*, and is a form of voluntary departure. However, administrative deportation is often ignored by the immigrants and rarely enforced by the authorities. The second form is 'forced deportation' which is exercised for security reasons and implemented under the Ministry of Interior. Under this form of deportation, immigrants are forcibly escorted to the border by authorities. The immediate effect of the *Legge Martelli* was increased number of deportations from Italy, the majority being forced deportations. The long-term effect was to further increase the exploitability of immigrant labour due to the lack of enforcement of administrative deportation; those immigrants who decide to ignore the deportation order become more dependent on the *lavoro in nero* as the Italian dual labour market continues to be organized along immigration status.

In 1991, the Albanian refugee influx made it difficult to implement the law due to the unprecedented volume of asylum seekers reaching Italy and the lack of infrastructure to process such a large number of immigrants in such a short time. (Mai, 2011). The government granted temporary residency to Albanian refugees and temporarily suspended the implementation of the law. Thus, similar to the *Legge Foschi*, the *Legge Martelli* lacked any consideration of integration of immigrants into Italian society and primary labour market. Although modified several times, the *Legge Martelli* remained in effect until 1998. During this time, the fragmentation of the Italian labour market increased, as both documented and undocumented immigrants increasingly occupied jobs in agricultural, domestic, and small industry sectors. For example, in 1994, 92.6% of all immigrants worked as *lavoro in nero* without legal contracts with largest sectors being: agriculture (27.5%), small industry (17.9%), and domestic workers (12.4%) (Magnini, 2012).

The *Turco Napolitano Law* that passed in 1998 presents five key changes. First, the law establishes the concept of "carrier liability" by creating an affirmative duty for the carrier to check the identity of the passengers. Second, it creates reserved quotas and regulates the inflow to Italy, giving preferences to immigrants coming from certain countries that have a bilateral agreement with Italy. Third, it creates *Centri di Parmanenza Temporanea* (CPT), which are holding centers where asylum seekers are held to establish their identity, originally for a maximum of 30 days. After 30 days, the applicant is released but the local authority is in charge of controlling the movement of the immigrant who is not allowed to leave a specified area and is brought back to the CPT in case of violating geographic restrictions. The fourth innovation is not to count refugees against immigration quotas. Unfortunately, the law does not specify a system to deal with asylum seekers but affirms that humanitarian and refugee issues are separated from immigration policy matters. Finally, the law makes an attempt to integrate immigrants, including those refugees and individuals granted subsidiary protection. This include the rights to family reunification as well as full access to the labor market, including some governmental positions, education and welfare assistance. Unfortunately, in spite of the efforts made by the law to implement refugee integration, the existence of a dual market and the permanence of *lavoro in nero* for immigrants is still a reality. As of 2002, both documented and undocumented immigrants were mostly concentrated in the agricultural, construction and domestic workers sectors with high exploitation both in terms of violations of work safety and remuneration. For example, the total income per month was less than EUR 440 for 2.1% migrant workers, between EUR 440 and EUR 639 for 19.1% of them, and between EUR 640 and EUR 839 for 26.4% of them. This suggests that immigrants are still concentrated in low-paid and precarious sectors of employment (Bich, Zanfrini, Zucchetti, 2006).

Therefore, the evolution of Italian immigration laws since the passage of the *Legge Foschi* in 1986 shows the failure of policies attempting to control immigration. Rather than controlling immigration, these policies have led to the emergence of a dual market where documented and undocumented immigrants are increasingly concentrated in low-paid and highly precarious employment with a significant percentage occupying positions of *lavor in nero* in the *economia sommersa*. An additional element of these laws has been their inability to promote social and economic integration of immigrants. To the contrary, they politicized the debate in immigration and fueled the emergency of populist and right wings groups, such as *Movimento Cinque Stelle* and *Lega Nord* (Bulli and Sorina, 2018). It is, indeed, populism that frames the next two reforms of Italian immigration laws.

The *Bossi-Fini* law amended in 2002 the *Turco-Napolitano* law by modifying the requirements to enter and remain in Italy and imposing stringent internal control. One of the most significant changes of this law is the contratto di soggiornolavoro (Residence Employment Contract). This is a mandatory employer-immigrant contract that ties the legal permanence of the immigrant to a labour and a rental contract. The law also provides the legalization of those employed as domestic helpers, including badanti, or as dependent workers provided they have a valid employment contract and have not received a deportation order. The law also imposes strict deportation practices by introducing, for the first time, detention for those seeking political asylum and extending the stays in the CPT to 60 days, renamed *Centri Identificazione ed Espulsione* (CIE). In 2009, the time of detention in the CIE is extended to 180 days and, in 2011, to 18 months. Moreover, immigrants found in international waters, formerly outside of the patrolling power of Italy, can be sent back to their country or to other countries and cannot dock on Italian coasts. The *Bossi-Fini* law was successful in expelling undocumented immigrants until in 2004 the *Corte Costituzionale* (Constitutional Court) declared direct expulsion as unconstitutional due to implementation without due process. After this decision, the percentage of expelled immigrants went down. The main effect of the *Bossi-Fini* law is to create a direct link between legal residence and employment. This increases the dependence of the immigrants on the employer since without an employment contract, the immigrant must either leave or become undocumented. Such dependence creates a condition of high exploitability for immigrants, especially undocumented and refugees due to their limited access to only *lavoro in nero*.

The political response to the 2015 refugee crisis[8] is framed within the principles outlined by the *Bossi-Fini* law especially in terms of deportation, patrolling of international waters and refusing docking to carriers of refugees. In 2017 the *Decreto Minniti* speeds up the application process for asylum seekers who are defined as a distinct category from unauthorized immigrants and are allowed to perform "voluntary work." Additionally, the *Decreto Minniti* rejects asylum seekers from a second appeal and tries to increase the numbers of CIE renamed as *Centri Permanenti per il Rimpatrio* (CPR) which should be located close to airports and far from the cities. This increases the isolation of immigrants and refugees alike and their position of vulnerability in the labour market. The 2018 *Decreto Salvini* and its 2019 amendments further increases the exploitability and vulnerability of immigrants and refugees by granting enhanced funds to law enforcement to both apprehend undocumented immigrants and individuals attempting to illegally enter the country and organized crime. The most relevant element of the *Decreto Salvini* is to abolish humanitarian grounds for refugee status. Under the *Decreto Salvini*, immigrants can be granted the status of refugee only if they are coming from war zones or are victims of human trafficking or other forms of egregious labour exploitation. By eliminating relief on humanitarian grounds, the law significantly reduces the number of immigrants who can be granted asylum.[9] Ultimately, the *Decreto Salvini* criminalizes the status of those already in Italy depriving them of basic rights and making asylum seekers more vulnerable to labour exploitation and organized crime.

In conclusion, Italian immigration laws have pushed immigrants to the lowest paid positions of both the *economia sommersa* and the primary economic circuit with sectors such as *badanti* and street vendors heavily occupied by foreign labour both in the primary and underground economy.

Turkey

In the early years of the nation-state building process, the Turkish Republic sought to erase the ethnic and cultural diversity of the Ottoman Empire and solidify a national identity based on Sunni-Islam and Turkish ethnicity (Sagiroglu, 2016; Kaiser and Kaya, 2016). In that vein, citizenship and migration laws were linked to religion and ethnicity (Yegen, 1999; Jongerden, 2007) and the legal framework was used as a tool for homogenization of the population

---

8 The refugees crisis of 2015 has put an undeniable strain over the cultural and economic infrastructure of Italy. For example, in 2017 according to data provided by the European Union, Italy had a total population of 60, 589, 445 of which 167,335 were refugees and 128,850 were asylum seekers. This was the second highest among EU countries second only to Germany with 222,560 of asylum seekers over a total population of 82,521,653 (EU Parliament, 2019).

9 For example, homosexuals facing prison time in Russia or adulterous facing the death penalty in Saudi Arabia or Iran cannot apply for refugee status.

(Kirisci, 2000). The 1923 Law of Migration and Resettlement (Mubadele, Imar ve Iskan Kanunu, no.368) was a generic law and did not specify any ethnic origins but religion, giving Muslim Bosnians, Albanians, and Tatars the right to settle in Turkey (Sirkeci and Pusch, 2016). The Settlement Law of 1934 (İskân Kanunu, no.2510) underlined ethnic origins together with religion, stating that the criteria for being accepted as an immigrant or refugee was "descending from Turkish ancestry or belonging to Turkish culture" (Sagiroglu, 2016, p.35). The 2006 Settlement Law (İskân Kanunu, no.5543) which substituted the previous one also excluded all persons who do not have Turkish origins, assigning the right to apply as an immigrant to only people with Turkish origins and/or ties. This legal framework still gives priority to people with ancestral links to Turkish ethnicity and culture in present-day Turkey.

Abiding by its legal framework and considering Islam as a significant aspect of the Turkish culture, the state displaced, resettled, or expelled non-Muslim minority populations and granted citizenship to exclusively Muslim migrants (Kaiser and Kaya, 2016; Sirkeci and Pusch, 2016) during the founding years of the republic. Within the country, non-Muslims were forced to pay the Wealth Tax (1942) and Kurdish populations in the east and south were forced to migrate (Kaiser and Kaya, 2016). In addition, 1932 Law on Activities and Professions in Turkey Reserved for Turkish Citizens (Türkiye'deki Türk Vatandaşlarına Tahsis Edilen Sanat ve Hizmetler Hakkında Kanun, no. 2007) regulated right to employment for non-nationals and forbid non-Turkish citizens to practice 72 professions, reserving those positions for Turkish Citizens (Pusch, 2016). Therefore, since the implementation of the first settlement law in 1923, Turkish immigration law has defined the citizenship rights along nationalistic and religious lines as well as facilitated emergency of a dual labour market by reserving primary sectors to Turkish citizens.

While the early period migrations resulted from nationalist ideologies and the Lausanne Treaty which implemented a compulsory ethnic population exchange, the migration regime and policies of 60s and 70s were linked to economic interests and focused on exporting large number of young, unemployed labour abroad. In 1961, the first bilateral labour exchange agreement with Germany started a new era in the Turkish migration history and made Turkey a country of emigration and source of labour for Germany, Austria, Netherlands, and Sweden in the following years (Sirkeci and Pusch, 2016; Kaiser and Kaya, 2016). These guest-worker agreements were the results of demographics and in line with the economic needs and policies of both receiving and sending countries, giving one side the legal framework for the opportunity of exporting excess manpower and to the other to import labour power. As a result, Turkish lower-level manual workers used their legal right to sell their own labour and filled the positions in the secondary sectors in receiving countries.

In 1980s, following the military coups and political upsurge, Turkey has become a major source country of political asylum seekers and thousands left for European countries. After 1980s, the country started to change its role over and receive migrant groups (regular migrants, transit-migrants, refugees, suitcase traders, circular migrants, and clandestine workers) from diverse ethnic and religious groups originating from Europe, former Soviet Union, Middle East, and Africa (major source countries being Bulgaria, former Yugoslavia, Iran, Iraq, Afghanistan, Somalia, and Syria) (Sirkeci, 2016). As a result of the shift in the migration flows and heterogenization of the composition of immigrants, the state's policy altered to focus on immigrants in the country. Besides, in 80s and 90s, the state was seeking entry into the European Union and adopting a new foreign-trade oriented economic growth strategy. In that context, Turkey was forced to adapt its migration legislation to meet the needs of economic and political globalization (Pusch, 2016) and fill the positions by foreign labour only when the demand is not met by the native population (Sirkeci, 2016). As a consequence, the 2003 Law on Work Permits for Foreigners (Yabancıların Çalışma İzinleri Hakkında Kanun, no. 4817) was implemented and the Law on Activities and Professions in Turkey Reserved for Turkish Citizens (Türkiyedeki Türk Vatandaşlarına Tahsis Edilen Sanat ve Hizmetler Hakkında Kanun, no 2007) which barred foreign nationals from working in 72 professions was abolished for immigrants with a legal work permit and status. However, the practice of specific positions such as engineer, architect, dental practitioner, lawyer is still prohibited for non-Turkish citizens (Pusch, 2016). The most important changes implemented by the law in regards to work permits are prioritizing the needs of the labour market, not nationality of applicants and opening work permits to individuals, not only companies (Icduygu, 2016).

Facing a large influx of people of non-Turkish ethnic origins and becoming host to the largest number of refugees in the world as a result of the civil war in Syria was a breaking point for Turkey to implement a Refugee Law. Even though Turkey had received many refugees since the early 20th century, its refugee regime was based on the ethnic origin and religion ideals of the nation-state and regulated by the 1951 Refugee Convention and 1967 Protocol, maintaining a geographical limitation and accepting responsibility of refugees to only coming from Europe (Sirkeci, 2016). Accordingly, while Turkish-origin and European individuals and families have been able to settle in the country, non-Europeans have been relegated as asylum seekers (instead of refugees) and permitted to stay in the country only for a limited time period with temporary protection status, with the hopes of receiving refugee status from other countries (Erdogan, 2015; Sirkeci, 2016). This refugee regime has left millions of non-European people, including Syrians, in the country without proper legal refugee status and work permit, creating a condition of vulnerability to exploitation in the labour market.

The Turkish government's first reaction to the Syrian crisis was to open its borders to civilians fleeing the war, place them in the refugee camps along the border, and provide protection and humanitarian assistance through some international NGOs and organizations. While this policy of open border and non-refoulment was highly praised by the international community, it had some legislative loopholes and administrative shortcomings (see Icduygu, 2015; Kaiser and Kaya, 2016; Yildiz and Uzgoren, 2016; Baban et al., 2017). First, Syrians were given a 'guest' status (specific to Syrians) which meant that they were expected to stay only temporarily and return after the end of the war. Second, the 'guest' status disqualified Syrians for applying to third countries as asylum seekers, trapping them inside the country. When the number of Syrian refugees increased rapidly in mid-2012, the government had to adopt new policies and permit more aid organizations to operate within the country. Formal procedures such as refugee registration and monitoring as well as activities, such as delivery of supplies and infrastructure and training healthcare workers, began after the realization that the crisis did not have a short-term end in sight. These conditions and pressure from the EU, who had the fear of Syrians coming to its borders, forced the Turkish state to reform its migration legislation. The process brought the first ever asylum law, the Law on Foreigners and International Protection (LFIP) (Yabancılar ve Uluslararası Koruma Kanunu, no. 6458) in 2013 which was entered into force on 11 April 2014.

The LFIB is regarded as a milestone as it formed the base for a new migration management. The new Directorate General for Migration Management (DGMM) was established within the Ministry of the Interior as the main entity in charge of policy making and proceedings for all foreigners, such as visa and asylum applications and integration of newcomers. The new law regulates the residency of foreign nationals in the country and introduces a long-term residence permit for foreigners who have stayed in Turkey for a minimum of eight years uninterruptedly. Concerning asylum seekers and refugees, the law for the first time, established a legal framework for this population and introduced regulations on International Protection. The law allows asylum seekers to apply for a work permit six months after their international protection claim, by identifying the restrictions (sectors, needs of the market at the time of application, etc.). While helping some refugees in the country, this law does not include Syrian refugees, who are the biggest refugee group in the country, due to their unique status (Icduygu, 2016).

The legislation, Regulation on Temporary Protection (RTP) (Geçici Koruma Yönetmeliği, no 6203) which was adopted in 2014 identified the rights and obligations for group-based 'temporary protection' for people who arrive *en masse*. According to this legislation, people arriving as big groups are under temporary protection and not eligible to apply for international protection. Therefore, while regulating the status of asylum seekers and refugees, the new law and its legislation has not solved the previous issues regarding the legal status and precarity of Syrians in the country. Foremost, Syrians are not granted 'refugee' status, but 'temporary protection', thus are not eligible to apply for asylum and resettlement in third countries as part of the international protection regime (Ineli-Ciger 2015) as they are not deemed to be in immediate danger (Baban et al., 2017). Furthermore, the UNHCR office, which is supposedly the main facilitator of asylum applications and resettlement, cannot register asylum seekers under temporary protection unless there is a specific need or family re-unification. DGMM identifies persons for resettlement and forwards to UNHCR after a multi-stage review and interview process of the referrals submitted by the provincial authorities in the country (UNHCR, 2018). "Since the start of the Syrian crisis to September 2018, UNHCR Turkey has submitted 56,702 Syrians for resettlement processing of which 27,478 Syrians have departed to the resettlement country" (UNHCR, 2018, p.3). Thus, the role of UNHCR is downsized to providing advice to the Turkish Government on refugee registration, camp management, assisting with voluntary repatriation and processing applications only for specific cases (Yildiz and Uzgoren, 2016). As seen, the government's current legal framework gives Syrians an ambiguous, temporary status besides does not implicate a path to permanent residency or citizenship (Kutlu, 2015).

Furthermore, the temporary protection status restricts the livelihoods of Syrians by permitting them to live in the cities they are registered, even though there is limited access to regular employment, education, social, and economic support in the cities crowded by Syrians. Today, Turkey is host to over 3.6 million (registered) Syrian refugees (UNHCR, 2019), under 10% of them live in refugee camps, the majority are dispersed throughout the country. Both camp and non-camp refugees are entangled in precarious living conditions with difficulty in finding work legally, maintaining strong social and economic networks, and establishing a secure life. They are biometrically registered (images and fingerprints) and subject to mobility controls through registration, headcounts, and security checks.

Moreover, the temporary protection regime and its legal framework puts Syrians in a vulnerable position in the labour market. According to the RTP and the Regulation on the Work Permit of Foreigners under Temporary Protection which passed in 2016 (five years after the arrival of first group of Syrians), people under temporary protection are not granted immediate right to employment, but can apply six months following their registration. Furthermore, the individuals' right to employment is to be determined by the Council of Ministers (acting on the advice of Ministry of Labour and Social Services) and is limited to specific sectors and geographical areas designated by the Council. According to the law, the application should be submitted by the employer who must show justification as to hiring a Syrian instead of a Turkish national and the number of Syrians cannot exceed 10% of its work force (Icduygu, 2016; Kutlu, 2015). Also, the employees cannot be paid less than the minimum wage, which creates equality, but hesitation for the employer to apply for the permit. These limitations and bureaucratic application process hinder access to employment rights and jobs for people under temporary protection. According to the labour statistics released by the Ministry of Family, Labour and Social Services (2016 and 2017), only 13,290 Syrians and a total of 73,549 foreigners were granted work permits in 2016 and 20,966 Syrians and a total of 87.182 foreigners in 2017, majorly in the sectors of manufacturing, construction, trade, service (food and beverage, accommodation), office and business support, education, and consultancy. Statistics show that majority of permits were definite (short term) and issued to applicants with a bachelor's degree or higher. The statistics do not differentiate between migrants, refugees, and people under temporary protection.

While the situation for people under temporary protection (mainly Syrians) is not favourable, a further law regulating employment of all foreigners in the country, the International Labour Force Law (Uuslararasi işgücü Kanunu, no: 6735) which was passed in July 2016 is also inspired by economic and national aspirations: "…the indefinite work permit should be mainly granted to foreigners who make investments that support the development of Turkey; are highly qualified foreigners who strive toward scientific and technological progress; are citizens of Republic of North Cyprus and other foreigners of Turkish descent who maintain strong linguistic, cultural and historic ties with Turkey" (Pusch and Sirkeci, 2016 p.14). This law employs a selective immigrant policy and outlines the required qualifications for prospective immigrants such as level of education level, professional experience, potential to contribute to science and technology and make investments. According to this law, foreigners can receive a work permit (Turquoise Card) that is valid for one year with a right to renew. After holding permits for a minimum of eight years, they have the right to apply for indefinite work permits and residency (Icduygu, 2016). As seen, recent migration policies have taken steps to attract highly skilled workers, increase productivity, improve trade and investment and facilitate economy (Sagiroglu, 2016).

In conclusion, the Turkish migration and asylum policies have been influenced primarily by the nationalist ideals of the state and reserved right to permanent settlement only to persons of Turkish descent and culture. Secondarily, they were shaped by the aspirations of the economy. In either way, the policies and legislation have facilitated and legitimized a segmented labour market, by classifying labourers in the market in parallel to their citizenship or immigration status, as legal or illegal persons to sell their labour in equal terms for definite or indefinite terms. Historically, immigrants with Turkish and European (but Islamic) origins have been recognized as legal persons who are entitled with rights, including the right to sell their labour and follow a path to citizenship. Non-Europeans seeking asylum on the other hand have been classified as the "other" who are entitled to stay in the country temporarily, therefore, not as subjects to the citizenship law or labour law. With recent regulations followed by large influx of refugees from non-European countries, the existence and needs of non-European asylum seekers are recognized. As a result, non-European asylum seekers and Syrians under temporary protection are allowed to apply for definite work permits, however, with several limitations and restrictions. Since Turkish policy is not to integrate them into the society in general and the primary sector of the labour market in particular, they are still deprived of basic rights to sell their labour freely and apply permanent residency or citizenship. By denying those rights, the legal framework forces refugees to highly precarious jobs in the secondary sectors within which they can serve as a reserve army of labour.

Discussion

The capitalist ideology asserts that employers and employees are free to meet at the labour market; mutually agree on rights and obligations; and outline those on a labour contract (Vercherand, 2014). This ideology is based on the ideals of "freedom" and "formal equality" of employers and employees. However, by identifying who has the freedom to participate in the labour market legally and equally, capitalist economies have found a way to justify unequal and unfree labour relations and exploit labour power. As discussed by Pashukanis (1924), labour is defined by the law as a commodity that is sold in the market in a legal form and only *free* persons are legally entitled to sell their labour as a commodity. Historically, some groups have not been defined as legal sellers of their labour, but only performers of the labour which turned them into commodities who can be sold in the market not by their selves, but their owners. Even though this contradicted the ideals of capitalist freedom and equality, by legally defining some people as legal objects (that can be sold), not legal subjects (who can sell their labour freely and equally), capitalism has justified the exploitation of their labour.

After the WWII, within western democracies labour exploitation was regulated by the differential treatment of migrant labour as defined by immigration laws. For example, the Bracero Program legalized the exploitation of rural workers in the US. Similarly, Gastarbeiter in Germany legalized the exploitation of workers from Italy, Spain, Greece, Turkey, Morocco, Portugal, Tunisia and former Yugoslavia to fuel the exponential growth of West German's economy in the 1950s. The uniqueness of these programs was the temporary status granted to the foreign workers, which created a condition of labour precarity. Moreover, these workers had no political rights, therefore, had no leverage in promoting changes. The current study argues that refugees are the new precarious labourers vulnerable to exploitation due to their temporary status and rightlessness.

This paper argues that the law legitimizes the exploitation of refugee labour, in a similar way to slave, indentured, and temporary worker labour, through limiting and illegalizing refugees' right to stay or right to sell their own labour freely in the market. The asylum and migration law determine the terms and conditions for participation of immigrants (asylum seekers, refugees, and migrants) into the labour market, thus their level of protection and precarity as a labourer. This way, the socio-legal migration status is used to segment the population and place in a social hierarchy and the persons' position in the labour market corresponds with that position in the social stratum. If the law defines a person as a 'migrant' with legal rights to reside and work, the migrant has the opportunity to sell his/her labour in the market freely and empowered to negotiate the conditions of selling his/her labour and join the protected labour. This migrant is assigned a legal status which comes with the power of negotiating his/her place in the labour market in particular and social hierarchy in general. For him/her, the negotiating power depends on the level of human capital. On the other hand, if the law defines a person as "temporary", "rightless," or "undocumented," it removes his/her power of contractual negotiation in the labour market by not recognizing the person as a legal subject. Regardless of his/her human capital and potential, the person is assigned a lower status in the labour market and the social stratification system. The level of negotiation power and degree of position in the social hierarchy will depend on the socio-legal migrant status that comes with varying rights, as a refugee, temporary protected (asylum seeker or guest), or undocumented; the undocumented having the least power and filling the lowest positions. That form of legal status forces the asylum seeker or undocumented who has the fear of deportation to sell his/her labour in the illegal economy and accept precarious conditions and terms.

The analysis of Italian and Turkish immigration law shows that the legal framework in those countries create vulnerability and precarity by entitling asylum seekers to none-to-limited rights. As explained above, immigrants in those countries are assigned various legal statuses with varying degrees of rights and power which allocate them to varying levels in the segmented labour market. With the aims of promoting brain gain, consequently economic growth, both countries accept migrants with high levels of human capital and grant them a higher status in the stratum (compared to other foreigners) through legal rights to work and reside. However, they have very strict policies when it comes to asylum seekers that arrive their borders. Even though both countries are signatories of the 1951 UN Convention, they adopt policies that violate or distort it. Turkey applies the rule of "geographical limitation" and recently its law defining "temporary protection for the people arriving in mass" as excuses not to grant rights to non-European asylum seekers while Italy tries to prevent entrance by eliminating the criteria on humanitarian grounds, refusing docking to carriers of refugees, sending back to safe third countries, and deportations. Implementing policies of 'closed borders' and 'temporary protection', these countries grant millions coming into their borders either no protection with a threat of deportation or temporary protection with no clear indication of a permanent status. The most defining reality of no legal status or temporary status implemented by Italy and Turkey is that of a legal framework that define asylum seekers as "others" who are expected not to integrate into the society, but to leave (on a determined or undetermined date). The legal framework takes away the right to freedom of movement, even for the asylum seekers with temporary protection. Moreover, asylum seekers are not recognized as legal persons who can freely sell their labour power in the labour market. With no-or-limited legal entitlements to employment, social welfare, or assistance, people are forced to live on savings as well as assistance provided by the NGOs or faith organizations in their regions. When their stay is prolonged, there is no argument that they must work in order to survive. However, the legal framework in both countries fail to address issues in regards to right to employment and protection, furthermore, strictly restricts the inclusion of asylum seekers in the formal labour market, particularly in the primary sector. This creates conditions of vulnerability and exploitability by employers, middlemen connecting refugees with employers and *the lavoro in nero* or work done without a labor contract. The outcome has been hiring under the table without contracts or protection which creates a segment in the labour market that is characterized by high level precarious jobs with very low payments, conditions, and security. Thus, instead of regulating employment, the current law generates an unregulated labour market within the already existing secondary labour market and legitimizes exploitation of asylum seekers/refugees within that market. Now, the secondary labour market gets divided into two segments; one defined with low level jobs for legal persons who are disadvantaged in the market due to their level of education, qualifications, or identity while the other is consisting of jobs with high levels of precarity and absence of protection by any forms of law. This lower and illegal segment of the secondary labour market gets to be occupied by vulnerable asylum seekers and others who are not recognized as legal persons by the law thus afraid to report poor conditions or abuse to authorities. Moreover, since the status of asylum applicants are defined and regulated by the asylum and immigration law, not the labour law, the state takes no responsibility of precarity or exploitation, maintaining the ideology of moral superiority of capitalist labour relations.

Furthermore, since asylum seekers/refugees are legally defined as 'others' with no legal or equal rights, their exploitation is not typically seen as an issue of the national labour market and their struggle is perceived as their own, as they are perceived as refugees, not as workers. This can be seen as the process of socio-legal construction of refugees as *'others'* which contributes to the expansion of precarious labour and increase in ethnic tensions in receiving societies. Deprivation of legal permanent status and basic rights such as access to employment (especially in the primary sector); being subject to 'otherization' and discrimination; and living with the constant fear of deportation create multiple vulnerabilities for refugees in both countries. Furthermore, the existence of refugees with no legal protection makes it possible for employers to use them as the reserve of army labour (Marx, 1867) and displace workers who are entitled to higher wages and safe working environments owing to their socio-legal status. Having no legal rights to sell labour or negotiate, asylum seekers/refugees are left with no choice but to accept precarious conditions, replacing previous workers. Consequently, this situation creates ethnic antagonism and class conflict amongst working class (Bonacich, 1972). Asylum seeker/refugee participation in the labour market creates discontent within the working class since the members of the host society starts to see them as competitors in the labour market and start to lose their jobs or protected conditions as a result of utilization of refugee labour as reserve army of labour and gives negotiation power to the employers. Moreover, that conflict fosters nationalistic rhetoric against immigrants, largely refugees, because the decline of protected labour is seen as a result of immigrants' participation in the labour market, not as a result of the dynamics of capitalist labour market and government mis-regulation. Consequently, both countries are susceptible to increasing levels of ethnic conflict in the coming years.

Conclusion

In sum, the current asylum system and refugee regimes are far from regulating the residence of asylum seekers, refugees, and undocumented (rejected asylum seekers) within receiving societies, but function to benefit the capitalist economies by creating a new vulnerable and precarious working class consisting of these groups. The general tendency of states to grant only temporary status or no legal status has created a condition of labour precarity that has fueled economic growth, by legitimizing the exploitation of refugee labour. Through an analysis of policies and legislation in two countries, this paper argues that current immigration laws delegate immigrants to various degrees of social class position depending on their immigration status and relegate asylum seekers and refugees to highly precarious and exploitable work. Keeping asylum seekers and refugees outside the labour law and defining them as "temporary" or "illegal" by using the migration law, the legal framework socially constructs refugees as *"others"* who have no rights to work or stay. At the same time, it fuels an anti-immigrant sentiment among the native labour force who perceives these refugees as the reason for their declining economic opportunities. The current situation cannot be resolved without a legal reform and constructive integration policies that expand immigrants' rights to access to free labour markets. The new asylum and migration policies need not only to consider the financial aspect of accepting refugees and providing humanitarian assistance, but also to start seeing prolonged refugees as long term, even permanent residents and develop comprehensive and sustainable integration programs to avoid economic, social, and security problems.

References

ACTRAV (2011). Policies and Regulations to Combat Precarious Employment. International Labour Organization

Baban, F., Ilcan, S. and Rygiel, K. (2017). Syrian refugees in Turkey : pathways to precarity , differential inclusion , and negotiated citizenship rights, Journal of Ethnic and Migration Studies, 43(1), pp. 41–57.

Bank, W. (2015). Turkey's Response to the Syrian Refugee Crisis and the Road Ahead, The World Bank Group. No. 102184

Ben-Ghiat, R. and Hom, S.M. (2015), Italian Mobilities, Routledge.

Berman, H. (1983). Law and Revolution: The Formation of the Western Legal Tradition. Cambridge, Massachusetts: Harvard University Press

Bichi R., Zanfrini L., Zucchetti E. (2006). Il Mezzogiorno dopo la grande regolarizzazione, Milano: Franco Angeli.

Bonacich, E. (1972). A theory of ethnic antagonism: The split labour market, American Sociological Review, 37(5), pp. 547–559. doi: 10.2307/2093450

Bulli G. and Sorina S. (2018). Immigration and the Refugees Crisis in a New Immigration Country: The Case of Italy. HKJU-CCPA, 18(1), pp.127-156

Carpio, X.V. Del.and Wagner, M. (2015). The Impact of Syrians Refugees on the Turkish Labour Market. Policy Research Working Paper. World Bank Group. No.7402.

Castles, S., Miller, M.J. and Ammendola, G. (2005). The Age of Migration: International Population Movements in the Modern World, New York: Guilford Press.

Donati, S. A. (2013). Political History of National Citizenship and Idenity in Italy, 1861-1950. Stanford, CA: Stanford University Press

Einaudi, L. (2007). Le politiche dell'Immigrazione in Italia dall'Uita` a Oggi. Bari (IT): Editore Laterza

European Parliament, EU Migrant Crisis: Facts and Figures. http://www.europarl.europa.eu/news/en/headlines/society/20170629STO78630/eu-migrant-crisis-facts-and-figures

Erdoğan, M.M. (2015). Türkiye'deki Suriyeliler: Toplumsal Kabul ve Uyum. Istanbul: İstanbul Bilgi Üniversitesi Yayınları.

Gramsci, A. (2005). The Southern Question. Toronto: Guernica Publisher

Huddleston, T., Bilgili, O., Joki, A. and Vankova, Z.D. (2015). Migrant integration policy index, Mipex. retrieved from: http://mipex.eu/sites/default/files/downloads/files/mipex-2015-book-a5.pdf

İçduygu, A. (2015). Syrian refugees in Turkey: The long road ahead, Washington, DC: Migration Policy Institute.

İçduygu, A. (2016). Turkey: Labour market integration and social inclusion of refugees. European Parliament, Directorate General for Internal Policies, Policy Department Economic and Scientific Policy. Study for the ASMPL Committee.

İçduygu, A. and Diker, E. (2017). Labour Market Integration of Syrian Refugees in Turkey : From Refugees to Settlers, Goc Arastirmalari Dergisi, Vol. 3 (1). pp. 12–35.

Ineli-Ciger, M. (2015). Implications of the new Turkish law on foreigners and international protection and regulation no. 29153 on temporary protection for Syrians seeking protection in Turkey, Oxford Monitor of Forced Migration, 4 (2), pp. 28–36.

International Labour Organization (2011). Policies and regulations to combat precarious employment. Geneva, Switzerland.Retrieved from: https://www.ilo.org/wcmsp5/groups/public/---ed_dialogue/---actrav/documents/meetingdocument/wcms_164286.pdf#targetText=Although%20a%20precarious%20job%20can,trade%20union%20and%20bargaining%20collectively.

Internatinal Labour Organization (2012). ILO Indicators of Forced Labour Introducing the Indicators. Geneva: International Labour office. Retrived from: https://www.ilo.org/wcmsp5/groups/public/---ed_norm/---declaration/documents/publication/wcms_203832.pdf#targetText=Introducing%20the%20indicators&targetText=These%20indicators%20are%20intended%20to,who%20may%20require%20urgent%20assistance.

IOM (2010). The Italy-Philippines migration and remittance corridor. http://publications.iom.int/system/files/pdf/italy_philippines_remit.pdf

Jongerden, J. (2007). The settlement issue in Turkey and the Kurds: An analysis of spatical policies, modernity and war. Leiden and Boston:Brill.

Kaiser, B. and Kaya, A. (2016). Transformation and Europeanization of Migration Policy in Turkey: multiculturalism, republicanism and alignment, in Turkish Migration Policy, eds. Ibrahim Sirkeci and Barbara Push. London: Transnational Press London, pp. 23–40.

Kirişçi, K. (2000). Disaggregating Turkish citizenship and immigration practices, Middle Eastern Studies,36 (3), pp. 1–22.

Kutlu, Z. (2015). From the ante-chamber to the living room: A brief assessment on NGO's doing work for Syrian refugees, Open Society Foundation. retrieved from: http://www.anadolukultur.org/en/areas-of-work/cultural-diversity-and-human-rights/from-the-ante-chamber-to-the-living-room/179

Magnani, N. (2012). Immigration control in Italian political elite debates: Changing policy frames in Italy, 1980s–2000s. Ethnicities, 12(5), 643–664. https://doi.org/10.1177/1468796811432693

Marx (1867). Capital. A Critique of Political Economy. Book One: The Process of Production of Capital Volume I. Progress Publishers, Moscow, USSR. English edition first published in 1887.

Mai, N. (2011). Reluctant Circularities: The interplay between integration, return and circular migration within the Albanian migration to Italy. Metoikos Project. European University Institute

Memisoglu, F. and Ilgit, A. (2017). Syrian refugees in Turkey : multifaceted challenges , diverse players and ambiguous policies, Mediterranean Politics, (22) 3, pp. 1–22.

Miggiano, A. (2015). The Iranian diaspora in Italy. Research in Iran and Iranian diasporas: Findings, experiences, and challenges. Proceedings of a Conference Sponsored by DĀNESH Institute, Inc. Bloomington (Indiana): Indiana University Center for the Study of the Middle East.

Nunez, D. (2013). War of the words: Aliens, immigrants, citizens, and the language of exclusion, BYU L. Rev., HeinOnline, p. 1517.

Pashukanis, E.B. and Arthur, C.J. (1978). Law and Marxism: A general theory, Vol. 5, London: Ink Links

Piore, M.J. (1979). Birds of passage: migrant labour and industrial societies. Cambridge England: Cambridge Univ. Press.

Pusch, B. (2016). (In)Compatible transnational lives and national laws: the case of German citizens in Turkey. Istanbul: Istanbul Policy Center, Sabanci University.

Pusch, B. and Sirkeci, I. (2016). Introduction:Turkish Migration Policy at a Glance, in Pusch, B. and Sirkeci, I. (Eds.), Turkish Migration Policy, Transnational Press London, pp. 9–22.

Sağıroğlu, A.Z. (2016). "Turkey's migration law and policy: is it a new era?", in Push, B. and Sirkeci, I. (Eds.), Turkish Migration Policy, Transnational Press London, pp. 41–54.

Sirkeci, I. (2016). "Turkey's refugees, Syrians and refugees from Turkey: a country of insecurity", Migration Letters, Transnational Press London, Vol. 13 No. 1, pp. 127–144.

Smith, A. (2000). The wealth of nations, eds. Edwin Cannan, New York: The Modern Library.

Togral, T. B. (2016). Syrian refugees in Turkey: from 'guests' to 'enemies' ?, New Perspectives on Turkey. Cambridge University Press: Vol.54. pp. 55–75. doi: https://doi.org/10.1017/npt.2016.4

UNHCR The UN Refugee Agency. (2016). Resettlement in Turkey, available at: https://www.unhcr.org/tr/wp-content/uploads/sites/14/2018/10/UNHCR-Turkey-Resettlement-Fact-Sheet-September-2018.pdf.

UNHCR The UN Refugee Agency. (2019). Syria Regional refugee response, available at: https://data2.unhcr.org/en/situations/syria/location/113 (accessed 18 June 2018).

Vercherand, J. (2014). Labour: A Heterodox Approach, Springer.

Yıldız, A. and Uzgören, E. (2016). Limits to temporary protection : non-camp Syrian refugees in Izmir, Turkey, Southeast European and Black Sea Studies,16(2), p. 195-211.

Legal Documents

Convention relating to the Status of Refugees (189 U.N.T.S. 150, entered into force April 22, 1954)

Decreto Salvini:
https://www.ansa.it/documents/1537814391766_dlsicurezzaeimmigrazione.pdf

Immigrazione: Testo Coordinato Decreto Minniti. https://www.sprar.it/wp-content/uploads/2017/01/immigrazione-il-testo-coordinato-del-decreto-minniti.pdf

Royal Decree No. 773 of 1931. https://www.refworld.org/docid/3ae6b52918.html

Constitution of the Republic of Italy, 22 December 194

Dublin III Regulation (previously the Dublin II Regulation and Dublin Convention); Regulation No. 604/2013

CHAPTER 2

HOW FAR DO MORAL VALUES SHAPE THE LEGAL TERMINOLOGY USED IN INTERNATIONAL CONVENTIONS CONCERNING MIGRANT WORKERS?

Sureyya Sonmez Efe

Introduction

The international labour migration is an important phenomenon for both migrant-sending and migrant-receiving countries. According to the International Labour Organisation (ILO) statistics, in 2017, migrant workers accounted for 164 million of the world's estimated 258 million international migrants (ILO, 2018). There are 234 million international migrants who are at working age which impacts on the ILO statistical data (ibid). The labour participation of migrant workers into global labour force (70.0 per cent) exceeds the total non-migrants' participation (61.6 per cent) (ILO, 2018). However, the statistical data does not reflect the number of irregular migrant workers who participate into global labour force undocumented without a legal status. Therefore, the percentage of migrant worker participation into the world labour force might well be higher than the official figures.

The ILO describes the term migrant worker as "…all international migrants who are currently employed or are unemployed and seeking employment in their present country of residence". In this statement the status of a migrant worker is described based on migrant's 'employment status' and economic activities whose root cause for migration can be economic or political or social. It includes 'all international migrants' which takes a broad approach to the status of a migrant worker as someone who joins the labour market of the host country regardless of his legal status under the state jurisdiction. Thus, according to the ILO definition, the legality of the status and the root cause of migration becomes irrelevant concepts for defining persons' migrant worker status. I concur with this approach in this paper where I argue that refugees, stateless persons and irregular migrants become migrant workers once they participate into the labour market of their residence (Sonmez Efe, 2017).

On the other hand, the inclusion of other categories under the term migrant worker shows that the issue of legal definition of migrant workers become more complex for policymakers at international and state levels. The statistical data demonstrates the significant number of migrants who are not legally defined as migrant workers; there are approximately 65.6 million forcibly displaced people, 22.5 refugees, 10 million stateless people worldwide who are indirectly and in some cases directly linked to labour migration (UNHCR, 2018). Forced migration is a growing global issue which has become endemic as a result of varying political, sociological, environmental and economic factors. Thus, the paper claims that it is becoming hard to estimate the number of unofficial figures of global migrant workers because migrants from various legal statuses mentioned above who become integral to the labour force of the host countries.

One of the reasons for the complexity of labour migration figures is the ambiguity of the definition/description of the status of migrants under states' jurisdictions. The term migrant worker and other statuses of migrants are defined within the international conventions, which mainly take a humane and comprehensive approach to the terminology used for the definition. However, the conventions are non-coercive which means the recognition and adoption of these legal statuses by state policies is voluntary. Thus, the states have freedom to make their own decisions on legal definitions, admissions, residence and rights of migrant workers under their jurisdiction. On the one hand, it is important that international conventions provide an appropriate legal guidelines for states to define status and rights of migrants (workers). On the other hand, the same conventions give freedom to states to choose and adopt a policy approach for migrant workers which can be selective or restrictive towards labour migration and migrant workers' right to freedom of movement.

In the contemporary world, states' policies are usually dominated by a terminology that adopts 'restrictive approach' to admissions, residence, and rights of migrant workers. States unwillingness for taking a rights-based approach to labour migration arguably contributes to this approach, which has become a globally accepted phenomenon. This paper suggests that the legal terminology concerning migrant workers adopted by international conventions plays a crucial role for states' policies approach taken under their jurisdiction. The analysis of the international conventions concerning migrant workers shows that labour migration and rights of migrant workers are treated as a separate case which is arguably mirrored to the states' policy attitude towards migrant workers. In this context, 'values' become crucial in defining the legal terminology concerning status and rights of migrant workers at international and state levels.

In this paper I claim that there is a lack of unified moral approach to the rights of migrant workers because International Law gives the states the full responsibility to design their own immigration policies. The paper suggests that state policies are social constructions and cannot be independent fully from political and social cultural norms of its national community. In this context, states have freedom to use national and/or moral values when designing their policies of admissions, residence and rights of migrant workers. Thus, I argue that socially constructed moral values are central in creating international conventions and conceptualising the status and rights of migrant workers. In other words, the values have a grave impact on the legal terminology adopted by the international conventions and are crucial in terms of recognition of the status of migrant workers and protection of their rights at state level.

The key objectives of the paper is to provide an analysis of the terminology used in international conventions concerning migrant workers within the framework of the concept of 'porous values' (Sonmez Efe, 2017); to identify the porous and/or impermeable values in international conventions; to address the moral approach taken by these conventions to labour migration and migrant workers; and to improve the rights of migrant workers through including a moral approach in the debates on labour migration.

The methodology of the paper comprises of a theoretical analysis of the legal terminology concerning migrant workers; and a qualitative analysis of the key international conventions that aims to study the inclusion/exclusion of the 'moral values' in definitions of the legal status of migrant workers. For the former, the paper takes (cosmopolitan) moral constructivist approach in its theoretical analysis which allows an inclusion of the 'concept of porous values' (Sonmez Efe, 2017) into the study of legal terminology adopted by international conventions that address international labour migration and rights of migrant workers. For the latter, the paper uses an empirical analysis of the conventions with the inclusion of the primary data derived from semi-structured interviews and participant observation collected for the PhD research titled 'Legal Rights of Migrant Workers in Contemporary Turkey' (ibid). The UN and ILO conventions concerning labour migration/migrant workers will be the key official documents for the analysis. The paper will include the relevant secondary literature into the analysis such as Sonmez Efe (2017), Carens (2013), Benhabib (2004), and Rawls (1989). The paper uses thematic analysis of the primary and secondary data mentioned above. This method has best suited for the paper in terms of bringing the focus of the paper into the case of labour migration/migrant workers in international conventions through the lens of moral values.

The conclusion of the analysis has three key points; first moral values have been and will be the key instruments for creating and shaping the international conventions. Second, both 'porous' and 'impermeable' values exist within international conventions that impact on the terminology adopted to define the status of migrant workers and lay down their rights. Third, labour migration is treated as a separate category which is reflected on the terminology adopted by the UN and ILO conventions in the concept of state responsibility for having a moral approach to labour migration.

Theoretical approach

The terminology concerning the status and rights of migrant workers is legally complex and politically contested issue for both states and individuals (Sonmez Efe, 2017, p. 8). Therefore, it becomes an imperative to take an interdisciplinary approach to analyse this issue that includes political, philosophical, sociological and economic arguments. The interdisciplinary approach is integral to the moral constructivist worldview which includes moral arguments into the analysis of procedures and laws. As mentioned above, this paper uses moral constructivism[1] (Timmons, 2003) derived from cosmopolitan constructivism of moral ethics which is defined as "moral judgements are to be true by the virtue of procedures and laws that are constructed by us, persons" (Sonmez Efe, 2017, p.8).

According to the constructivist worldview individuals and institutions give subjective meanings to their understanding of rights which are influenced and formed through historical and cultural norms and interaction with others; and these meanings and understandings are created and negotiated by social actors and institutions (Berger and Luekmann, 1967; Lincoln and Guba, 1985; Crotty, 1998; Mertens, 2010; Lincoln et.al. 2011 cited in Creswell, 2014, p.8; Sonmez Efe, 2017, p.8).

Persons and procedures are key elements of law-making process according to moral constructivism and 'values' sit at the core in terms of influencing and shaping the terminology used within laws. In this context, 'persons' are defined as "…free and equal people…capable of taking part in social co-operation as capable of acting reasonably and rationally" (Rawls, 1980, p.518).

Thus, persons are defined with the values of 'freedom, equality and morality' (Sonmez Efe, 2017, p. 11). As moral constructivist worldview takes a universalist approach to define persons, these values become the attributes of all human beings regardless of their legal status of residence. In other words, moral persons are members of universal moral community as well as of the community of state where cross border movements of these persons are a part of the procedures (ibid, 12). This view recognizes the interconnectedness of the communities of states and claims that state borders are fluid concepts that are constructed by us, persons. These borders are not only simple lines appear on the map, but they are also laden with meanings and understandings that we, persons created through our experiences, history and shared values. The state borders can be inclusive for outsiders to enter which is described by Benhabib (2004) with the concept of 'porous borders' which explains cross border movements with porousness of state borders. According to this concept, people are allowed by state laws to become members of the host community (2004).

In this paper I claim that porous borders require 'porous values' (Sonmez Efe, 2017) which become a source for inclusive and moral immigration policies. 'Porous values' are constructed by moral persons; are flexible that allow non-members into a community of state; dynamic that are prone to transformation based on conditions; encompass cosmopolitan moral values of respect, dignity, worth and human being; are not restrictive based on ethnocentric boundaries

---

1 Some of the moral constructivist reading of Kant from contemporary literature are Benhabib (2004), Carens (1996, 2015), Habermas (1998), Held (2010), O'Neill (2004), and Rawls (1989).

(Sonmez Efe, 2017, 80). Figure 1 maps out the impact of the values on law making process and legal terminology:

Figure 1: The impact of the moral values on the law making process and legal terminology.

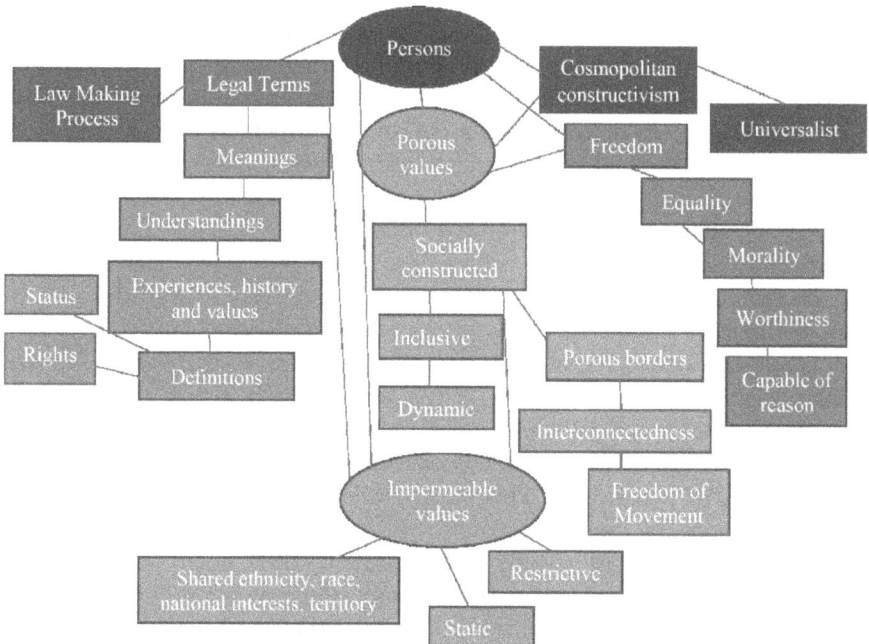

Source: The Figure is derived from the Diagram 1: The relationship between persons, procedures and values in studying policies concerning rights of migrant workers (Sonmez Efe, 2017, p.10).

Figure 1 illustrates how this paper articulates the relationship between moral values, law-making process and definitions used in policies concerning rights of migrant workers. As discussed above, we, persons create and attribute meanings to the terms that define our identity, legal status, rights, membership to a community and borders of our nation. These meanings are integral to the law-making process at international and state levels that are entrenched in the legal terminology that we use to define one's status and rights. Values that are porous allow these meanings to be flexible and dynamic where persons are capable to enter and exit to a community using their autonomous agency. In this context, the concept of porous values recognizes that every individual is a human being, capable of reason, have value in himself and worthy of respect (ibid). With these attributes persons are capable of reason which enables them to be a part of law-making process as well as to be subjects of the law. In the context of labour migration, porous values allow policymakers to make sense of the meanings and understanding that is attributed to the legal terminology that define the status of migrant workers and lay down their rights in the host community. It is to allow them to take an inclusive approach to migrant workers' freedom of movement and membership rights. According to this concept, freedom of movement is a universal human right that ought to be recognized by all communities.

However, there also exist values that are restrictive and exclusive to non-members' membership into a host community which I call 'impermeable values' (ibid, 79). These values define one's membership status based on (and limited to) shared ethnicity, ideal of traditional nationalism and common values of jus sanguinis (ibid) which can be discriminatory against non-members entry and admission into a host community. As opposed to porous values, impermeable values are static and aim to preserve the meanings and understandings of the terms to define one's status and rights. These terms are created based on collectivity, shared history, ethnicity, race, national interests, territory and sense of belonging. All these attributes allow persons to develop their identity within a given community, however, they can also be restrictive to outsiders' membership to this community. As Anderson would describe it these values are imagined (Anderson, 2006) and socially constructed with the inclusion of impermeable values which decides on one's membership statuses under the host country's jurisdiction. This paper recognizes the fact that impermeable values impact on the legal terminology of the nation states' immigration policies, however, it also claims that these values must be morally justified the reasons for exclusion of others from membership status and rights. The moral approach requires states to present a moral justification to their every action in law making process. The inclusion and/or recognition of porous values will allow such moral justification possible at policy level.

The paper also recognizes the impact of internal and external conditions on decision-making and law-making process at international and national levels. These conditions can influence the cause of migration, such as economic, environmental, conflict, personal choice of life. Cause of migration becomes crucial in legal and sociological definition of the status of migrants in the host countries, for example, one can be called as a migrant worker if the cause of migration is an economic one. However, I argue that the definition of one's status is more complex than this and one can become a migrant worker whether the cause of migration is an economic one or not. In this context, a refugee, asylum seeker or a stateless person can become a migrant worker if/when he/she is engaged in remunerated activity in the host country's labour market. Thus, the paper particularly focuses on the status of migrant workers and recognizes the complexity of defining one as a 'migrant worker' based on the cause of migration. The question is whether we call one a 'migrant worker' who migrate into another country for economic purposes, or someone from another legal status who also actively join the labour market of the host country. In other words, it is important firstly, to clarify whether it is the legal status that determine the laws that define one as a migrant worker or the cause of migration; secondly, to analyse how values (moral, national, universal) contribute to the definition of the legal status a migrant worker. The paper suggests that legality cannot be taken as only category for defining someone as a migrant worker, other internal and external conditions are also needed to be taken into consideration. Thus, the legal status of migrant workers cannot be determined merely based on one subject area, there is need for inclusion of other disciplines in studying status of migrant workers such as economy, sociology and politics.

Thus, the theoretical approach of the paper emphasises on the need for an interdisciplinary approach to the analysis of legal terminology concerning migrant workers within International Law. The paper argues that the values are integral to the law-making process and have an impact on legal terminology for defining the status of migrant workers. It builds the theoretical arguments of 'porous values' on moral constructivism which locates values at the core of persons and procedures that are the key elements of law-making process. It is the values that impact on the legal terminology of the immigration policies of the states and international conventions concerning migrant workers. The section also includes the internal and external conditions that influences the cause of migration for migrants in terms of making life-changing decision on their lives; and impacts on legal definitions of one's status based on international conventions and state policies.

International conventions

This section analyses the definition of the status of migrant workers within the key International Labour Organisation and United Nations Conventions concerning migrant workers. It discusses the inclusion/exclusion of moral values on their approach to the status and rights of migrant workers and how it impacts on national policies. The section attempts to identify the porous and impermeable values that exist within these conventions.

International Labour Organisation (ILO):

The ILO takes a moral approach to the labour rights based on three key principles; social justice, decent work and universality (Sonmez Efe, 2017, p.88). The term 'social justice' is defined by the ILO as

all human beings, irrespective of race, creed or sex, have the right to pursue both material well-being and their spiritual development in conditions of freedom and dignity, of economic security and equal opportunity (1944).

This statement from the ILO Declaration of Philadelphia and the ILO Constitution (2012b) advocates all human beings' right to decent life and freedom of movement within the concept of social justice. This ILO principle aims to inspire the policy of the member nation states on the fair treatment and fundamental rights of all human beings. It is important to emphasise that the Declaration does not spell out the term 'migrant worker', however, it uses the term 'human being' which is an inclusive term that encompass migrant workers too. This broad definition does not mention 'legality' or 'nationality' as key binding conditions for these rights.

A similar broad definition of a migrant worker comes from an ILO Official that is interviewed during the fieldwork analysis in Turkey in 2015. The interviewee uses a comprehensive definition of a 'migrant worker' which takes various conditions into consideration to define a migrant worker;

people who voluntarily or involuntarily work and live in a country other than their own are defined as migrant worker…there are subcategories of this status and it has a heterogenic character….the reason for migration can be an economic one, but also cultural one…forced migration, trafficked persons, refugees, asylum seekers, undocumented migrants…all of which has to sustain a decent living economically in the host countries…who want to empower themselves economically (The ILO Official, 2015).

The statement clearly shows the complexity of defining the status of migrant workers. The terminology that is used also shows the contemporary ILO approach to the definition of migrant worker which is inclusive where the cause of migration can become irrelevant to call someone a 'migrant worker'. The contemporary ILO approach supports the irrelevancy of the purpose of migration when categorising workers as 'migrant workers within its statistical data;

The concept of international migrant workers is meant to measure the current labour attachment of international migrants in a country, irrespective of the initial purpose of migration, and of others who are not usual residents of the country but have current labour attachment in the country of measurement. In this context, the terms 'international migrant workers' and 'international migrant and non-resident foreign workers' are equivalent. They are defined, for statistical purposes, as all persons of working age present in the country of measurement who are in one of the following two categories: (a) usual residents: international migrants who, during a specified reference period, were in the labour force of the country of their usual residence, either in employment or in unemployment; (b) not usual residents, or non-resident foreign workers: persons who, during a specified reference period, were not usual residents of the country but were present in the country and had labour attachment to the country, i.e., were either in employment supplying labour to resident producer units of that country or were seeking employment in that country. (ILO, 2018, p. 1).

In this statement, the ILO focuses on two key areas when explaining the concept of 'international migrant worker' within its data and report; employment activity, and legal status. For the former, the distinction made between an 'employed' and 'unemployed' international migrant worker where migrants' labour commitment and contribution into the host country becomes a value for their temporary or permanent membership. For the latter the differentiation is made between 'usual residents' meaning 'legal residents' and 'unusual residents' meaning 'illegal/irregular residents' which also uses two distinct terms to describe these categories; for legal residents it uses 'international migrants' whereas for illegal residents the term 'foreign worker' is used. On the one hand, the ILO recognises the presence and contribution of irregular migrant workers with the inclusion of the non-resident foreign workers into the international migrant worker category. On the other hand, the terminological variations that the ILO makes are akin to states policy attitudes to regular versus irregular labour migration dichotomy which is an integral part of their immigration policies.

The principle of social justice sits at the core of the ILO approach to labour rights which encompasses migrant workers. The key values that are mentioned are 'equality' and 'economic empowerment' within this principle. Moreover, the ILO formulated 'decent work agenda' in 2013 which aims to improve and protect individuals' well-being, development and dignity (Sonmez Efe, 2017, 88). According to the decent work agenda; "all individuals who are involved in remunerated activity including migrant workers fundamentally have the right to decent work and social protection" (ibid, p.89).

The decent work agenda encompasses the Declaration on Fundamental Principles and Rights at Work both of which promote elimination of all forms of forced labour, child labour, discrimination at work and right to collective bargaining (ILO, 2013C). The data from interviews also confirms the ILO's approach to the rights and protection of migrant workers;

the international norms say that…documented or undocumented migrants ought to have right to education and health care…fundamental rights…right to shelter…without any restriction, discrimination these migrants who work in the host country's labour market must be given equal rights with the local labour…these workers ought to have all the labour rights that native workers enjoy (The ILO Official, 2015).

The statement is important in terms of illuminating the values that are entrenched within the terminology used for laying down the rights of migrant workers. The interviewee takes an inclusive approach to the rights and protection of migrant workers based on the principles (or values) of 'equality', 'non-discrimination', and 'human being'. The paper considers these principles as 'porous values' according to which migrant workers are valuable based on the possession of intrinsic worthiness within themselves.

The universality principle promotes the good treatment of all people encompassing every state in the world regardless of their diverse social, political and economic capacities. The cosmopolitan world order rests upon the practice of democracy and inter-state dialogue and cooperation. Although, the existence of undemocratic states arguably becomes hindrance for a universal dialogue that promotes cosmopolitan values, the need for global cooperation on the issues like migration is an undeniable fact of the current world order. Such cooperation is not applied under a coercive mechanism as cosmopolitan system of justice is centred around democratic norms. In other words, it is a voluntary cooperation of the states on the global or local issues. Hence, the principle aim of the ILO is not to coerce its principles within conventions on the states' jurisdiction top-down, on the contrary, it aims to promote the universal values and to support governments to find solutions to labour problems that exist under governmental structure (Sonmez Efe, 2017, p.88). However, the paper claims that this type of approach has both top-down and bottom-up elements of governance and cooperation; the former approach aims to carry out a dialogue with governments which in turn will make a change from top-down at policy level; the latter is aimed through a creation of 'universal culture of rights' that is possible with collaboration not only with the governments but also non-governmental organisations.

The analysis of the ILO constitution and the key ILO conventions and recommendations[2] demonstrates the usage of language of rights for migrant workers. The ILO Constitution does not clearly define the status of migrant worker, however, the inclusive nature of its key principles, such as protection and equal treatment apply to workers who reside in the countries other than their own. The term 'migrant for employment' is mentioned in the ILO Convention No.97, however, it makes a clear distinction between regular and irregular migrant workers which is against its principles of non-discrimination and equality. The status of migrant worker is not defined clearly in the Convention, however, the inclusive language is used which also encompass the migrant workers. The analysis of the ILO Conventions and Recommendations clearly shows that the existence of migrant workers is recognized within states' labour markets, however, the ILO only focuses on the protection and rights of regular migrant workers which does not discuss the irregular migrant workers. In this paper, I argue that irregular migrant workers are also integral to the informal economy of the states, who also needs to be recognized as part of global labour force; not only within the statistical data as mentioned above, but also within the key principles of the ILO conventions.

The paper argues that the fundamental principles of the ILO are predominantly stemmed from moral values that are porous. The analysis of the key documents allows this paper to collate the key moral (porous) values when defining the status of migrant workers and laying down their rights; 'protection', 'equality', 'inclusion', 'respect', 'non-discrimination', 'decent work' universality and 'dignity'. All these values are reiterated and promoted throughout the ILO conventions and therefore have a grave impact on the status and rights of migrant workers at state level. Some of these conventions do not clearly define

---

[2] The ILO Convention concerning Migration for Employment No.97 (1949b); the ILO Convention No.111 on Discrimination (1958); ILO Recommendation Ro86 Migration for Employment (1949c); The ILO Recommendation R.100-Protection of Migrant Workers (Underdeveloped Countries) (1955); the ILO Migrant Workers Recommendation R.151 (1975B); the ILO Convention No.143 (1975);

the status of a migrant worker status, however, the ILO conventions use 'human being' which is a cosmopolitan value and includes migrant workers because of its universal nature.

The analysis of the ILO conventions also demonstrates that there are some elements that allows impermeable values to prevail within these conventions. Firstly, the emphasis on the 'legality' of the status of migrant workers impose a restriction to irregular migrant workers to have any rights at all within the host country. In this context 'legality' becomes an impermeable value that decides upon definition of migrants' status and impacts on their rights. On the one hand, the universality of the ILO principles enables a creation of a universal culture of rights which requires all nation states to adopt and implement the universal values to all human beings under their jurisdiction. On the other hand, the ILO recognizes the complexity of the world system where individual states have strong sovereignty which means their freedom of decision-making is also acknowledged. This entails difficulty in implementation of the principles of the conventions provided that individual states ratify the conventions voluntarily and adapt the ILO values within their jurisdiction. Thus, the states that are not subject to the ILO conventions are not bound to these universal values which means they can implement restrictive policies on migrant workers' entry, admission, status, and rights under their jurisdiction. This means, states are also free to include impermeable values into their policies particularly concerning irregular migrants and low skilled migrant workers.

Thus, the analysis of the ILO official documents shows the impact of the moral (porous) values on the key conventions and recommendations concerning labours and migrant workers. However, the implementation of these universal values at state level remains a problematic issue as a result of the emphasis on the legality of these workers made by the ILO conventions and the incompatibility between national values[3] of the states and universal values of the ILO.

United Nations (UN)

The legal terminology of rights used in International Law has been improved with the creation of the key Human Rights (HR) conventions; the International Covenant on Economic, Social and Cultural Rights (ICESR, 1966a); and the International Covenant on Civil and Political Rights (ICCPR, 1966B). The UN approach to the rights of all human beings are founded on the principles of 'universality', 'protection', 'human dignity', 'worthiness' and 'human autonomy and agency' all of which resemble the cosmopolitan moral values (Sonmez Efe, 2017, p.99). The inclusiveness of economic and social rights (ESRs) are

---

[3] 'National Values' are not included into the analysis in this paper as the paper mainly focuses on the impact of the values on migrant workers' rights within International Law. The impact of 'national values' can be discussed in a separate academic paper which requires to include an analysis of one or more case studies to illuminate such an impact. The PhD Thesis 'Legal Rights of Migrant Workers in Contemporary Turkey' (Sonmez Efe, 2017) looks into the national and regional values which can be covered within a separate paper.

prominent in the UN principles where moral entitlements of every individual are recognized merely because he/she is a defied as 'human' (ibid).

However, the UN conventions make a distinction between ESRs and civil and political rights (CPRs) which influence the states and individuals' perception of these rights as not being equally important. The fulfillment of the CPRs by the states is emphasised more as having a primary importance than the implementation of the ESRs where the fulfilment of the latter is bound to the states' economic conditions. This approach has a grave impact on the states' perception of the ESRs which are not given the same value as the CPRs. One reason for the perception of the hierarchy between ESRs and CPRs is that it is claimed that ESRs does not require moral urgency whereas CPRs does. For example, this type of distinction views one's protection from torture as more important than one's right to social security (Cranston, 1973). This paper acknowledges the treatment of some cases with the principles of urgency, however, it disputes the hierarchy between the ESRs and CPRs because the principle of social justice and rights is more complex than such a crude distinction. In other words, ESRs and CPRs are intertwined and needs to be taken similar care and moral treatment at international and state levels. For example, decent living standards are key for empowerment of an individual in economic terms which prevent their exploitation within the labour market is equally important with prevention of torture; as one's exploitation by an unscrupulous employer in informal market can fall under the definition of torture as a result of impact on the employee' psychological and physical well-being.

Another problem with the aforementioned distinction is the broad perception of ESRs as not being universal because it is claimed that not every human being is considered as an employee (Cranston, 1967 cited in Minkler, 2013, p.367). This is a weak argument as universality of rights is not founded on the utilitarian principles of maximization of happiness of greater numbers. It does not only encompass group rights, it includes the claims of individual rights too. Thus, ESRs ought to be recognized as universal rights because economic well-being is an important condition which impacts upon all individuals whether they have employee status or not. I argue that the dichotomy made between CPRs and ESRs has a grave impact on the perception of policy-makers on rights of migrant workers. This is evident from the low ratifications (51 signatories[4]) (UN, 2018) of the UN convention on Rights of Migrant Workers (ICRMW) which encompass elements from both CPRs and ESRs. Another reason for the low ratifications is arguably as a result of the inclusive character of the convention which includes all migrant workers within its scope irrespective of their legal status within the host country (regular and irregular migrant workers) which is arguably considered as a problem for

---

4 51 countries ratified the ICRMW most of which are from underdeveloped, developed, upper-developed countries. None of the chief industrial countries have ratified this convention which arguably could be due to the hierarchy made between ESRs and CPRs as ICRMW is considered to fall under the scope of ESRs.

implementation of rights to all migrant workers under host states' jurisdiction.

The analysis of the ICRMW confirms the UN's inclusive approach to the definition of the status of migrant workers; "…a person who is to be engaged, is engaged or had been engaged in a remunerated activity in a State which he or she is not a national" (1990, p.876).

The key determinants of the status are the economic activity and legality (nationality) which does not explicitly make a distinction between regular (documented) and irregular (undocumented) migrant workers. It is a comprehensive definition that considers anyone as a migrant worker who is engaged in economic activity in a host country labour market. According to the ICRMW, the purpose of migration is not a determining factor for defining someone as a migrant worker. Moreover, the Convention recognizes and addresses the vulnerability of irregular migrant workers (Article 5, ICRMW, 1990) and their families (ibid, Article 4). In this context, 'recognition', 'inclusion' and 'protection' are key values that impact on the definition.

The ICRMW exclude the status of 'Refugee', 'Asylum Seeker' and 'Stateless Persons' from the scope of its definition of a migrant worker as there are separate UN conventions that cover rights of individuals from these legal statuses. However, I argue that this is incoherent with the definition of a 'migrant worker' mentioned above. The individuals from refugee or asylum seeker or stateless status who become a part of labour force of a host country become migrant workers de facto, because they participate and contribute to the economy of the host country with their economic activity.

On the one hand, the legal distinction between categories made in International Law enables states to have clear policies to protect individuals from each category based on their specific needs. On the other hand, such distinction entails a division between values that impact on legal terminology used to define each category. For example, state policies tend to use moral values (such as protection) and take more humane approach to the rights of refugees, but they use economistic values (such as human capability and skills) and take more restrictive approach to migrant workers (Sonmez Efe, 2017). For the case of former, the cause of migration of refugees is evaluated to be as involuntary or forced act which compels state policies to treat these migrants morally and humanely. For the latter case, the act of migration is economic and assumed to be a voluntary act which arguably justifies the states' restrictive policies to migrant workers' admissions. The clear and inclusive definition of the status of migrant workers recognizes the existence of irregular migrant workers in labour markets. However, it is also imperative to recognize that the ICRMW ought to include the complexity of the cause of migration which makes it difficult to explain it through 'international labour migration' and 'international migration' as two distinct categories.

The analysis of the fieldwork data shows that states' attitude to ESRs discussed above resonates their approach to labour migration where policies usually adopt economistic values to the legal terminology concerning migrant workers (Sonmez Efe, 2017). The paper claims that the treatment of 'labour migration' as a separate category of international migration arguably impacts on states' adoption of pure economistic values to labour migration. As discussed in the theory section we, persons, attribute meanings and understandings to the legal terminology for defining status and rights of migrant workers. Therefore, the meaning of labour migration and the status of migrant workers is given by the persons who are capable of drafting international conventions and state policies. These meanings are constructed with the influence of the values that are entrenched in national communities, such as ethnocentric national values; and external conditions, such as political conflicts and economic crises. The ICRMW is founded on the moral values, however, the argument in this section demonstrates that the convention indirectly allows national values that impact on the legal terminology used in International Law. With this impact, the ESRs are arguably considered as secondary importance; national interests become central for labour migration; citizens' interests and rights exceed the rights of migrant workers; the distinction between labour migration and other forms of migration is made; and the complexity of the cause of migration is overlooked. There are also external conditions that impact on international migration which also creates migrant workers with various legal statuses.

At this point, it is important to study labour migration through an interdisciplinary approach which enable the researchers to make sense of the cause of migration that is an evolving phenomenon. This paper argues that

the inclusion of moral values within legal terminology to define status of migrant workers in international and national laws is important for the elimination of all forms of discrimination (Sonmez Efe, 2017, p. 105).

This approach considers the act of migration as an intrinsically humane act therefore it recognizes the need for a humane policy approach to labour migration which is based on the principle of 'non-discrimination'. Inclusion of moral values into the decision-making process will arguably enable the policymakers to revisit the pre-existing meanings and understandings of terms that create boundaries for freedom of movement; such as 'sovereignty', 'territory', security' all of which are broadly used within the contemporary migration literature (Sonmez Efe, 2017). A UN Official that is interviewed also points out this issue with the following statement;

There is no reason why states have this absolute power, it has started to be eroded after the Human Rights paradigm after the Second World War but it is still very much in the belief of the state apparatus that it can do whatever it likes. And…this is something that we collectively need to get rid of because it serves no purpose. There is no need for states to be sovereign, there is certainly need for military decisions, security decisions taken at one, in one place but it is not, it should not be out of sovereignty, it should be out of mandate, given the mandate to protect people, and they should be attached to accountability. And that is true for cities, that is true for provinces like…in Canada, Quebec has a big role to play, it holds budget in education and health by provincial in Canada, so in election at provincial level is very important often more important at federal level, so all these territories that matter and…in that sense nationalism should die' (2015).

The statement does not dismiss the need for the existence of the security and military provisions at national level, however, it emphasizes on the 'state accountability' and duty to protect people. This statement arguably promotes porous borders and the need for more regional alliances which can have a positive effect for regional migratory movements. In this era, there are more regional alliances which shows the evolution of the concept of nationalism where states recognise the interconnectedness of world politics and economy. International migration is the evidence of the interconnectedness of world communities which requires states to reinvent the concepts of 'sovereignty', 'territory' and 'border'. The UN is arguably a democratic platform for the states to have a dialogue on the global issues like migration and rights. It is also an intergovernmental institution which lays out moral principles for that advocates freedom of movement and protection of migrant workers. The inclusion and promotion of porous values by the UN is crucial for international dialogue and cooperation of states on labour migration; and for being an inspiration policymakers at state level.

Thus, the section argued that the UN conventions fundamentally take a moral approach to the status and rights of migrant workers which uses universal values that are porous. This approach considers every individual as 'human being' with 'dignity' and 'worthiness'. The section also argued the problematic areas of the UN conventions that indirectly allow impermeable values infiltrate in their legal scope, such as ethnocentric (national) values and territorial boundaries.

Conclusion

The paper analysed the legal terminology used in international conventions concerning status and rights of migrant workers. It was to see to the impact of values on the legal terminology which has been studied within the framework of the concept of 'porous values' (Sonmez Efe, 2017). The paper focused on the ILO and UN conventions on labour migration and migrant workers and aimed to address their approach to labour migration, and to identify the porous and/or impermeable values used in these conventions and migrant workers. After the analysis, the paper can conclude that both ILO and UN conventions take moral approach to labour migration and protection/rights of migrant workers. The paper argues that values definitely have a grave impact on the legal terminology used to define the status of migrant workers by the ILO and UN where both organisations include 'porous values'; human being, social justice, protection, equality, respect, dignity, agency, autonomy, worthiness, democracy, non-coercion, non-discrimination. All these values are reiterated several times within the ILO and UN conventions concerning migrant workers.

However, there are three key areas within the international law allow

---

Sonmez Efe

impermeable values within the conventions to prevail. Firstly, the international law makes a distinction between the CPRs and ESRs where latter rights are seen as secondary moral urgency which arguably goes against the principles of universality of rights, non-discrimination and equality. I argued that such a distinction made within international conventions influences the states' attitude to the rights of migrant workers as the ICRMW encompasses both ESRs and CPRs principles.

Secondly, another distinction is made between labour migration and international migration which is arguably reflected on the states' attitude to labour migration. The non-coercive character of the international organisations with regard to ESRs partly is the cause for the states' restrictive attitude to labour migration. States are given a full responsibility on adoption and implementation of the principles of the conventions concerning migrant workers under their jurisdiction. This means and entails a voluntary cooperation of states on the issues of migrant workers. Non-coercion is a vital cog of the cosmopolitan system of justice which has a democratic platform. However, the lack of a unified universal moral approach to labour migration becomes a hurdle against the recognition of freedoms and rights of migrant workers.

Thirdly, the international conventions that are analysed make a clear distinction between the categories of migrants where the status of migrant workers is one of them. It is argued throughout the paper that when we include the internal and external conditions that impact on the cause of migration, we can conclude that it is difficult to make a clear-cut distinctions between the migrant categories. I argued that the status of migrant workers is one of the most problematic categories in this regard. The legality is the central part of the distinction which pushes irregular migrants outside of the scope of protection and rights.

Thus, the ILO and UN conventions are crucial in terms of enabling and including the porous values within its legal terminology; promoting universal moral values; advocating human rights; cooperating with states for adoption and implementations of the moral principles. The ILO and UN stand as a democratic platform for such cooperation to prevail. However, the aforementioned problematic areas within both organisations shows the need for the reinvention of some universal terms that impact on the status and rights of migrants/migrant workers. This in turn will arguably improve the rights of migrant workers under states jurisdiction through an inclusion of a moral approach in the debates on labour migration.

References

Anderson, B. (2006). Imagined Communities. New York: Verso.

Benhabib, S. (2004). the Rights of Others: Aliens, Residents and Citizens. United Kingdom: Cambridge University Press.

Berger, P.L., & Luekmann, T. (1967). The social construction of reality: A treatise in the sociology of knowledge. Garden City: NJ. Anchor.

48

Carens, J. (1996). Realistic and Idealistic Approaches to the Ethics of Migration. International Migration Review, 30 (1), 156-70.

Carens, J. (2013). The Ethics of Immigration. New York: Oxford University Press.

Creswell, J.W. (2014). Research Design: qualitative, quantitative and mixed method approaches. UK, India and Singapore: SAGE.

Cranston, Maurice (1967). Human Rights, Real and Supposed. In Minkler L. (2013) The State of Economic and Social Human Rights: A Global Overview. The USA: Cambridge University Press.

Cranston, M. (1973). What are Human Rights? London: Bodley Head.

Crotty, M. (1998). The foundations of social research: Meaning and perspective in the research process. Thousand Oaks: CA. Sage.

Habermas, J. (1998). The Inclusion of the Other: Studies in Political Theory, trans. C. Cronin. Cambridge, Mass.: MIT Press.

Hasenau, M. (1991). ILO Standards on Migrant Workers: The Fundamentals of the UN Convention and Their Genesis. International Migration Review, 25(4) pp. 687-697.

Held, D. (2013). Principles of Cosmopolitan Order. In: Brown, G. W. and Held, D., (eds.)The Cosmopolitanism Reader. Cambridge: Polity Press.

ILO (International Labour Organisation) (1944). Declaration of Philadelphia. ⟨https://www.ilo.org/wcmsp5/groups/public/---asia/---ro-bangkok/---ilo-islamabad/documents/policy/wcms_142941.pdf⟩ [Accessed 18 March 2019].

ILO (International Labour Organisation) (1949b). CO97-Migration for Employment Convention (Revised) Available from ⟨http://www.ilo.org/dyn/normlex/en/f?p=NORMLEXPUB:12100:0::NO:12100:P12100_ILO_CODE:C097⟩ [Accessed 4 November 2013].

ILO (International Labour Organisation) (1949c) Ro86-Migration for Employment Recommendation (Revised) Available from ⟨http://www.ilo.org/dyn/normlex/en/f?p=NORMLEXPUB:12100:0::NO:12100:P12100_ILO_CODE:R086⟩ [Accessed 13 July 2015].

ILO (International Labour Organisation) (1955). R100-Protection of Migrant Workers (Underdeveloped Countries) Recommendation. Available from ⟨http://www.ilo.org/dyn/normlex/en/f?p=NORMLEXPUB:55:0:::55:P55_TYPE,P55_LANG,P55_DOCUMENT,P55_NODE:REC,en,R100,/Document⟩ [Accessed 3 November 2013].

ILO (International Labour Organisation) (1958). C111-Discrimination (Employment and Occupation) Convention. Available from ⟨http://www.ilo.org/dyn/normlex/en/f?p=NORMLEXPUB:12100:0::NO:12100:P12100_INSTRUMENT_ID:312256:NO⟩ [Accessed 3 November 2013].

ILO (International Labour Organisation) R151 (1975b). Migrant Workers Recommendation. Available from ⟨http://www.ilo.org/dyn/normlex/en/f?p=NORMLEXPUB:12100:0::NO:12100:P12100_ILO_CODE:R151⟩ [Accessed 12 June 2015].

ILO (International Labour Organisation) (1975). C143-Migrant Workers (Supplementary Provisions) Convention. Available from ⟨http://www.ilo.org/dyn/normlex/en/f?p=NORMLEXPUB:55:0:::55:P55_TYPE,P55_LANG,P55_DOCUMENT,P55_NODE:SUP,en,C143,/Document⟩ [Accessed 12 June 2015].

ILO (International Labour Organisation) (2012b). ILO Constitution. Available from ⟨http://www.ilo.org/dyn/normlex/en/f?p=1000:62:0::NO:62:P62_LIST_ENTRIE_ID:2453907:NO#A7⟩ [Accessed 30 October 2013].

ILO (International Labour Organisation) (2012c). ILO Constitution Preamble. Available from ⟨http://www.ilo.org/dyn/normlex/en/f?p=1000:62:0::NO:62:P62_LIST_ENTRIE_ID:2453907:NO#A4⟩ [Accessed 2 November 2013].

ILO (International Labour Organisation) (2013b). About the Governing Body. Available from ⟨http://www.ilo.org/gb/about-governing-body/lang--en/index.htm⟩ [Accessed 27 October

2013].

ILO (International Labour Organisation) (2013c). ILO Decent Work Agenda. Available from ⟨http://www.ilo.org/global/about-the-ilo/decent-work-agenda/lang--en/index.htm⟩ [Accessed 3 November 2013].

ILO (2018). Global Estimates on Migrant Workers: Results and Methodology. Available from <https://www.ilo.org/wcmsp5/groups/public/---dgreports/---dcomm/---publ/documents/publication/wcms_652001.pdf> [Accessed 18 March 2019].

ILO (2018). Labour Migration. Available from <http://www.ilo.org/global/topics/labour-migration/lang--en/index.htm> [Accessed 1 June 2018].

Lincoln, Y.S., & Guba, E.G. (1985). Naturalistic inquiry. Beverly Hills: CA. Sage.

ICRMW (International Convention on the Protection of the Rights of All Migrant Workers and Members of Their Families) (1990). Available from ⟨https://treaties.un.org/pages/ViewDetails.aspx?src=TREATY&mtdsg_no=IV-13&chapter=4&lang=en%20on%202%20November%202013⟩ [Accessed 20 October 2013].

Lincoln, Y.S., Lynham, S.A., & Guba, E.G. (2011). Paradigmatic controversies, contradictions and emerging confluences revisited. In: Creswell, J.W. (2014) Research Design: qualitative, quantitative and mixed method approaches. UK, India and Singapore: SAGE.

Mertens, D.M. (2010). Research and evaluation in education and psychology: Integrating diversity with quantitative, qualitative and mixed methods. 3rd edition. Thousand Oaks: CA. Sage.

O'Neill, O. (2004). Autonomy, Plurality and Public Reason. In N. Brender and L. Krasnoff (eds.) New Essays on the History of Autonomy. Cambridge: Cambridge University Press.

Rawls, J. (1989). Themes in Kant's Moral Philosophy. In: E. Förster (ed.) Kant's Transcendental Deductions. Stanford: Stanford University Press.

Sonmez Efe, S. (2017). Legal Rights of Migrant Workers in Contemporary Turkey. Unpublished doctoral thesis. Leeds Beckett University.

Timmons, M. (2003). The Limits of Moral Constructivism. Ratio, XVI: 391-423.

UN (2018). UN Treaty Collection: International Convention on the Protection of the Rights of All Migrant Workers and Members of their Families. Available from <https://treaties.un.org/Pages/ViewDetails.aspx?src=IND&mtdsg_no=IV-13&chapter=4&lang=en> [Accessed 7 June 2018].

UNHCR (2018). Figures at Glance. Available from [http://www.unhcr.org/uk/figures-at-a-glance.html> [Accessed 1 June 2018].

CHAPTER 3
A HUMAN RIGHT TO RELOCATE: THE CASE FOR CLIMATE MIGRANTS

Melina Duarte

Introduction

Human rights are abstractly defined as the basic set of fundamental rights and freedoms owed equally to every person by virtue of being human. At its core, human rights are supported by the idea of human dignity, freedom, justice and world peace (UN 1948, Preamble). Human rights law aims at rendering this ideal more concrete by enacting a universal code that regulates the state's actions towards individuals and groups (UN 1948, Preamble). The code aggregates a series of basic civil, political, economic, cultural and social rights that are meant to be protected irrespective of race, color, sex, language, religion, political or other opinion, national or social origin, property, birth or other status (UN 1948, art. 2).

Since the Universal Declaration of Human Rights was adopted as the foundational code (UN 1948), the body of human rights law have been expanded in order to more specifically address the disadvantages suffered by women (UN 1979), children (UN 1989), disabled persons (UN 2007), members of minority groups such as racial minorities (UN 1965) and, to some extent, refugees (UN 1951). Expanding the body of human rights law, however, is not a simple task. Sometimes it is not even a desirable one. Not every social demand, for example, can or should be enshrined in human rights law (Freeman 2011, 6). Excessive expansions can overemphasize the view that the rights are relative or contingent and lead to the idea that whereas some rights need to be protected, others need not be. Inclusions can also conflict or undermine the observance of other already-acknowledged rights. Furthermore, if the proposed expansion is too aspirational, it might weaken the regulatory function of human rights and make it harder to hold states accountable for observing them. Thus, in proposing an expansion of human rights law, one has to be careful not to trespass some boundaries that would lead to more harm than good in terms of promoting the protection of people's rights. To the extent it is possible, a proposition for expanding human rights protection should be able to show that (1) the proposed right carries enough moral weight to be universalized, (2) it does not conflict with the majority of the already acknowledged human rights, and (3) is not excessively aspirational (see Miller 2016a, 11-31).

This paper will focus on the first condition by arguing that a right to relocate for climate migrants carries enough moral weight to be turned into a human right and therefore be included in human rights law. Section 2 starts with some conceptual clarifications. Section 3 sets the basic premise of the argument by assigning to human rights the function of protecting our distinctive human capacity that is, in Griffin's terms, our normative agency. Section 4 shows that the vulnerabilities of climate migrants are currently not acknowledged and not addressed within the framework of human rights. Section 5 seeks to unveil these vulnerabilities and show that they are strong enough to disrupt the climate migrants' agency capacity and thus degrade their humanity. Section 6 proposes to restore the climate migrants' agency capacity by granting them a human right to relocate. Section 7 concludes. The argument is, however, not complete because the second and third conditions for proposing an expansion of human rights protection are not discussed in this paper.

Conceptual clarifications

Relocation is, in general lines, understood as the process of moving from one place to another. When we organize our wardrobe, for example, we are probably relocating some clothes from one compartment to another. Animals can be relocated from the zoo back to nature. Traveling to a holiday house on the summer is also to relocate from place A to place B. This means that the term "relocation" refers, in principle, to any transfer from place A to place B that contains the idea of a stop, sojourn, or settlement at place B. The term is, in this sense, neutral and does not say anything about what triggered the movement itself. It also does not imply that a person's ties with place A are interrupted when relocated to place B, nor that place B is her final destination. This paper, however, is concerned with a particular type of relocation that emerges in response to forced displacement. This type of relocation is different than others because "displacement" implies that the shift in location was compelled or induced by another factor, i.e. that the relocation is not voluntary, but provoked by a serious disturbance at place A that makes living there undesirable or unbearable. Many factors can produce this effect. It is not immediately clear which factors imply duties to assistance and entitlements for compensation and it is even less clear who should be required to deliver this assistance or compensation. War and conflicts are currently the most prominent example of what is called "forced displacement" generating these claims. Because people are forced out of their homes due to war and conflicts, they are entitled to be assisted in order to preserve their human rights in a situation of aggravated vulnerability (Carens 2013, 195; Gibney 2004, 233; Miller 2016b, 83). There might be disagreements about what a duty of assistance might entail, e.g. positive or negative duties, but overall we can say that states, at least the signatories of the 1951 Refugee Convention and its 1967 Protocol, acknowledge some kind of duty towards refugees. The duties of signatory states towards refugees are underpinned by three principles: non-discrimination, non-penalization, and, most fundamentally, non-réfoulement. Respectively, these principles prevent states from disfavoring some groups of refugees over others, from criminalizing border crossing by asylum seekers, and from sending refugees back to the place they are fleeing from. Natural disasters, many of them caused by human activities, are another factor that, though still largely underrepresented in human rights law, displace millions from their homes, forcing them to relocate. Even though the number of displacements caused by slow-onset natural disasters such as rising sea-levels, droughts, and land degradation remains unknown, sudden-onset natural disasters such as storms, flooding and tsunamis are already displacing more people than war and conflicts – a rate of one person every second (Bronen and Pollock 2017). Since 2008, an annual average of 21.5 million people have been displaced by sudden-onset disasters (UN 2016). These high numbers are expected to increase considerably in the near future due to the intensifying impacts of climate change (McAdam 2017). The magnitude and scope of the issue lends support to the claim advanced in this paper by showing that climate migration will virtually affect the life of everyone on the planet, either on the sending or receiving side. A human right to relocate for climate migrants would then entitle them to move and resettle in another location. Which location? In some (or even most) circumstances, the conditions are such that the relocation can be done within the state's borders. However, in others, people must relocate abroad in order to reach safety. In principle, a human right to relocate for climate migrants would consist of an entitlement to move and resettle irrespective of whether this involves border crossing or not. However, given that domestic freedom of movement is an already acknowledged human right, the defense of a human right to relocate in this paper focuses on the conditions that make a right to relocate abroad emerge. A right to relocate for climate migrants in such conditions equals, in this sense, a right to immigrate under planned and collective conditions.

Defining climate migrants, let alone being able to apply such a definition to identify climate migrants in the real world, is not an easy task. The available literature is full of controversies and inconsistencies (e.g. Nicholson 2017, 49-66; Gemenne 2017, 394-404). As a political philosopher, I am well aware of the conceptual difficulties, but believe that a lack of agreement on the terminology should not stop us from engaging in this pressing debate. Conceptual clarity is of course important, but a consensus might never be reached and in order to tackle such issues we need to proceed from some preliminary, even if imperfect, concepts (see conceptual discussion at Neuteleers 2011). Considering all of this, my working definition is as follows: climate migrants are persons whose migration is driven by sudden or slow changes in the environment leading to a significant degradation of their lives and living conditions, independently of whether these environmental changes have already occurred or are predicted to occur in the future (see baseline definition IOM 2011, 33,). Since climate change cannot be easily singled out as the only or the main reason provoking actual or imminent displacement apart from socio-economic and political reasons, applying such a definition for identifying climate migrants in the real world must rely on additional guidelines. In order to fulfill that purpose, we must perhaps accept that every person fleeing from areas that are already suffering or will, according to predictions, suffer substantial damages from the impacts of climate change should be considered a climate migrant.

For specific cases in which forced displacement has already occurred as a result of an actual disaster, I reserve the subset term of "climate refugees". Such specification, however, should be done with great caution in order to exploit its analytical value. The refugee crisis sparked in 2015, for example, revived a debate around whether, contrary to refugees, migrants were not forcibly displaced and as such did not deserve special mobility and assistance concessions (Nair 2017). Furthermore, legally speaking, forced displacement is not enough to determine whether someone deserves such special entitlements or not. Due to the rather narrow scope of the 1951 Refugee Convention and its 1967 Protocol focusing more on what caused vulnerabilities than on the vulnerabilities themselves, to be forcibly displaced is only legally meaningful if one is forcedly displaced for the right reasons which involves persecution or an internationally recognized and substantial inability of a state to take care of its citizens and residents in cases of war. Climate change is not currently among these reasons. Such uses of the term "climate refugees" and of the distinction between climate refugees and climate migrants is somehow problematic. This is the case because, first, the distinction can be understood in terms of a conceptual opposition instead of conceptual agreement and, second, because the term "climate refugee" seems to be legally meaningless. "Refugee", however, is not mutually opposed to the concept of "migrants" nor an exclusively legal term. The analytical value of using both concepts, however, is not in assigning a different moral obligation towards each, but in making it clear that if we fulfill our moral obligations towards climate migrants, we might prevent many of them becoming refugees. Every climate refugee is a climate migrant, though not every climate migrant is or must become a refugee. Whereas, at the policy level, the protection of climate refugees would function in post-disaster settings, the protection of climate migrants would also encompass pre-disaster settings. Thus, by advancing the case for climate migrants in general, I expect to show that despite the different circumstances, at least when climate is one of the drivers of migration, both climate migrants and climate refugees suffer from similar vulnerabilities resulting from imminent or actual forced displacement that equally deserve attention. I intent to bring forward the vulnerabilities emerging from imminent displacement and evaluate how much they affect our distinctive human capacity, i.e., our normative agency. If these vulnerabilities happen to be significant enough to deprive climate migrants of their humanity, there will be grounds for saying that a right to relocate for them carries enough moral weight to support including a new human right in human rights law.

I introduce another definition in order to emphasize both poles of mobility, the sending and the receiving side, i.e. the definition of climate migrant receivers. This definition is important because a human right does not mean only an entitlement to right-holders but also an obligation to duty-bearers to respect, protect, and fulfil such a right. Climate migrant receivers are, in this sense, those on the other end, bearing the duty to accommodate climate migrants. Even if in reality, some states will minimize their role as actual climate migrant receivers by negotiating that climate migrants should be relocated to other states, and even if some individuals will minimize their role as climate migrant receivers by preferring climate refugees to resettle in another neighborhood, it is important to emphasize that from the point of view of climate justice, every state or individual should have a proportional and equitable duty to be a climate migrant receiver. Establishing a human right to relocate then requires showing that the claims of climate migrants hold enough moral weight and significance to justify an imposition of such a duty on climate migrant receivers. And this is the first and perhaps most important condition that a proposition for a new human right must meet.

Agency-based account on human rights: Protecting normative agency as our distinctive human capacity

In order to analyze and verify whether the climate migrants' claim for a human right to relocation carries enough moral weight to impose a duty on climate migrant receivers, we can start by scrutinizing the basic justification of human rights. In general terms, human rights are justified as providing a code for protecting what fundamentally determines our status as human beings (e.g. Forst 2012; Griffin 2000). The protection of what determines our status as human beings overrides the states' national agendas and citizenship rights. Griffin (2000, 32) argues that our status as human beings emerges from our distinctive capacity of "deliberating, assessing, choosing, and acting to make what we see as a good life for ourselves" — i.e., to be a human being is essentially to be the agents of our own lives. For him, to be an agent, one must (1) be able to choose one's own path throughout life without being dominated or controlled by others (autonomy); (2) make choices that are, what he calls, "real", i.e. informed choices that enable conscious acting (minimum provision); (3) and not be forcibly prevented from pursuing what one sees as a good life (liberty) (Griffin, 2000, 33). We might choose not to subscribe to Griffin's agency-based account for the justification of human rights. However, even if it can be argued that protecting our normative agency, as our distinctive human capacity, is not the only function of human rights and that Griffin overvalues it when attempting to ground every human right directly or indirectly on agency (Liao 2009, 15-25), it is difficult to argue that agency plays no role in justifying human rights. Accepting this premise at its most basic level is not, in this sense, controversial. In order to move forward, we now have to ask whether the vulnerabilities of climate migrants are of such a sort as to disable or disrupt their agency capacity at a level strong enough to degrade their humanity and whether the human right to relocate would be able to restore this capacity.

Climate migrant vulnerabilities are not acknowledged and therefore not addressed

For bringing such vulnerabilities to light at a more nuanced level, it might be helpful to consider a hypothetical case of a climate migrant in concrete terms. Tina is a climate migrant. At the moment, she has a job, a house, a structured family and a rich network of meaningful relationships with friends, colleagues, neighbors and co-habitants. She happens to live in a territory that is going to be severely distressed by the impacts of climate change. Part of her state's territory will become inhospitable for human living, but some areas will remain habitable. Predictions vary considerably regarding when this will happen, but there is fairly broad agreement that it will. Although the leaders of her state are aware of the problem and willing to take action, her state does not have enough resources to build a whole new infrastructure capable of avoiding, diminishing or even delaying the territory loss. Furthermore, even if her state, with massive international help, manages to do something, due to practical and financial limitations, it is very unlikely that the scale of the project would be large enough to make her or the resettlement of her co-habitants entirely dispensable. At some point, Tina or her offspring will have to relocate. Resorting to the already recognized human rights related to freedom of movement, what are her options?

As her first option, empowered by the human right to domestic freedom of movement (UN 1948, art. 13.1), Tina could move to the remaining areas of her state and attempt to reestablish herself there—which would characterize internal displacement. This, however, might not be a good idea if many others from her densely populated state are doing precisely the same thing. At some point, the remaining areas might not be large enough to accommodate and support all displaced persons. Data on the displacements from Syria, for example, shows that the refugee crisis was an outcome of a previous crisis of internal displacement suggesting that cases of massive internal displacement can evolve into cross-border displacement. How to determine when one more inhabitant becomes too much for a territory seems to become a crucial question. This question could be posed in terms of food or job availability, for example, but also in the simple terms of physical space. The problem is that even supposing that we are able to answer this question in a as fair and exact way as possible, the worse signs that a territory is unable to support its residents such as the lack of drinkable water or the inability of producing food, for example, do not currently generate a right to relocate abroad. Take the case of Malawi, where the responses to severe deprivation of most basic goods leads, at most, to the delivery of humanitarian help in loco, but it does not generate a right to its citizens to relocate abroad. So, for Tina it seems that as long as her state has a remaining portion of land considered habitable and a state representing her and her people, she would not have a strong claim when applying for relocation abroad. This is the case even if she struggles to reestablish herself on the overpopulated and impoverished land that is left. This problem becomes a real concern when, according to the predictions, the territories that will be most severely afflicted by climate change are located in highly populated low or lower-middle-income countries, such as Bangladesh, China, and India (Kintisch 2009; Poncelet 2009; Oliver-Smith 2011).

Alternatively, empowered by the human right to exit the afflicted land (UN 1948, art.13.2), Tina could consider crossing the border of her state to settle abroad. The problem with this option is that the right to exit does not grant Tina a correlative right to entry. In order to acquire permission to enter she would have to apply for entry using the ordinary schemes of migration. She can apply for a visa to immigrate to a specific state as a worker or investor, as a student, as a close family member of someone who already made the journey legally, and so on. In all these cases, however, a permission to immigrate is made at the discretion of the receiving state in consequence of its sovereignty and can either be granted or rejected. This means that by choosing this option, Tina would be left with no guarantees of success. She must accept that the odds of having her application rejected are high if she fails to meet any of the demanded criteria. Even if she were successful in her application, it is not guaranteed that she will be able to bring her extended family with her, nor that her neighbor next door would share the same success. Another problem is that, by attempting to migrate via these ordinary schemes, she is actually dissimulating the real reason of her migration, as if she were not forced to leave her place.

In order not to be entirely at the mercy of the receiving state, Tina could then attempt to migrate as a refugee and so be protected by refugee rights, having, at least, the right not to be returned to the afflicted territory (UN 1948, art.14 and also The 1951 Convention Relating to the Status of Refugees and 1967 Protocol). The problem with this route is that, legally, Tina does not yet qualify to be considered a refugee since (1) her territory has not yet disappeared from the map and might not even disappear completely and (2) climate alone is not yet and perhaps will never become a reason grounding asylum. To indisputably be considered a refugee, she would have to wait until she can prove that the instabilities in her home state have become serious enough to spark conflicts that put her life and freedom at risk, thus generating an immediate need to relocate. At the end, opting for this route would not only endanger her life, but also put everything that is meaningful in her life at risk. What Tina needs is the assurance that she, her family, and her people will be able to relocate in safety and the current set of human rights are failing to provide her that.

None of the current human rights to freedom of movement are satisfying for Tina because, as a climate migrant, she is in a transitional category, i.e. no longer a voluntary migrant because her displacement is not voluntary and not yet a refugee because her displacement is neither abrupt nor complete. Despite the partial loss of her territory, she still has a state that represents her and it is not technically being persecuted by it. In Rancière's terms (2000), she is what is called a "part of sans-part", i.e. a part of those whose voices are not rebutted, but inaudible; whose presence is not criticized, but invisible; whose rights are not denied, but unqualified. As such, Tina is among those who are not part of the excluded, but of the non-existent, because the institutional framework fails to acknowledge her status. In order to vindicate her inclusion to an institutional framework, we have to show how being a no longer or a not yet means, in some sense, being— it means becoming. This status shows that her vulnerabilities and the vulnerabilities of climate migrants are still invisible and the obligations towards them still need to be exposed. In order to disclose the special features that place them in such transitional category, we have to move forward and unveil their vulnerabilities.

Unveiling the main vulnerability of climate migrants: The loss of normative agency

Predictions show that Tina's territory will be severely compromised by the intensification of the impacts of climate change and that not only some parts of her state, but several other parts of the globe will become uninhabitable. These predictions are based on reliable evidence and are now relatively uncontroversial. It does not really matter when the loss of territory will occur; at this point, it does not really matter if it will occur at all. What matters is that she and others have reasons to believe in the predictions. The predictions then become a sentence. The relationship that she has had with her territory has already changed with the sentence and this severely affects her agency. Let us try to bring such changes to light with a thought experiment:

Imagine that you discover that your house has irreversible structural problems. The beams are all rotten. The most skilled carpenters have said that there is nothing that can be done. One day, it might be tomorrow or in a few years, the house will collapse. Would you still paint the walls, do the gardening properly, decorate the rooms carefully, build the swimming pool you always wanted, as if the house would not collapse? Would a bank give you a mortgage to renovate the facade and build your swimming pool with security on the house? Would someone who wants a house to live in buy this house from you? Now, imagine that on the top of that, knowing that your house will collapse, you were prevented to move out and relocate to a new house. What if you are left with no better alternatives but to live in a place that is about to collapse? At that very point, the problem is not a break with the past, but a disruption of the line of continuity connecting your past, present, and future provoked by the changing of meaning that the space you occupy and connect with now suffers. Prevented to relocate to another house, you become unable to forge new memories and new perspectives for your own future. It is then an end without restarting. Left with no alternative to move out and relocate to a new space with open possibilities to frame a new future, you become neither placed not displaced, stuck in a transitional end in space and time and, to a large extent, depleted of what makes you human, i.e. your normative agency.

The main point of this exercise is to show that being in a transitional category in which one's vulnerabilities are not acknowledged and therefore not addressed depletes one's agency capacity to direct one's own life. Although no analogy is perfect, I expected the personal reflection to intuitively capture the very moment when these unacknowledged vulnerabilities arise—i.e. the very moment in which one suffers the consequences of a harm before the harmful event actually happens. Yet, precisely because the harmful event has not yet actually happened, the consequences suffered are not acknowledged and not remedied. Between these stages is a kind of catch-22 situation in which in order to get better, one has to expect to get worse. When the house was sentenced to collapse, it triggered a chain of negative consequences. Some of these consequences can be the same or very similar to the consequences of the event of the house actually collapsing. As long as the house is still standing, it does not matter if it is about to fall apart, one cannot access the channels of assistance for the homeless. In order to access these channels and not become homeless, one has to become homeless.

By transposing the outcome of this thought experiment to the case of climate migrants, we can see that the predictions of the loss of their territory works as a sentence for them. This means that, independent of what actually happens to their territory and when, the prediction is enough to alter the connection that they have with a territory in a meaningful way, thereby creating a significant loss of agency that needs to be tackled. The prospects of losing their territory ends up making any further investment, emotionally and financially, pointless. That territory, being first a space that they occupied physically, was also a space of their agency that is now disrupted. It is the space where they built memories and made plans that shaped and gave meaning to her and her family's lives in the present. The threat of losing this space combined with having no perspectives for replacing it before they actually lose it, stagnates their agency in a transitional position wherein their capacity for framing their future is taken away from them. If we then go back to Griffin's agency-based account on human rights, we see that while in such a transitional category, climate migrants have their distinctive human capacity put on hold. Forcibly prevented to relocate to another place, they are unable to choose their own path through life and have no autonomy to frame their own lives; they are unable to make informed choices because no possibility is open for them; and they are unable to pursue what they see as a good life for themselves and have no liberty. In this sense, restoring their agency means restoring their status as members of humanity and this endeavor is worthy of an inclusion of a human right in the body of human rights law.

Restoring the normative agency of climate migrants

Assuming that we all agree that it is of fundamental importance for climate migrants to restore the normative agency lost by the prediction of losing their territory, there are two ways this could be achieved: (1) by removing the threat of losing their territory or (2) by allowing/facilitating their relocation to a new and safe territory. Opting for the former route, one would have to either engage (1.1) in some form of climate change denial, or (1.2) in some form of technological optimism, presuming that technology will be able to secure the territory by rectifying the changes caused by global warming. Both options are, however, unreasonable from a factual standpoint. (1.1) First, so much research shows the effects of climate change, one can no longer deny it without ignoring causal relations. (1.2) Second, although technology is a powerful tool for adaptation, one cannot realistically expect it to be powerful enough to entirely avoid the consequences provoked by climate change and completely remove the threat of losing territory for all persons affected by the predictions. The scale of the projects would have to be massive in order to promote some effects. Practical and financial limitations make it an unreliable option for the majority of people. What is then left is to rely on the latter route, i.e. (2) the one that consists in restoring the conditions of agency for climate migrants by allowing/facilitating their relocation to a new and safe territory irrespective of whether this involves border crossing or not.

Under the current regime, states regulate which territories can be occupied and by whom, but there are limits to how exclusive they can be both in material and non-material ways. Materially, states are faced with incentives why it is beneficial for them to support the inclusion of a human right to relocate for climate refugees. Non-materially, they are faced with a duty to support such an inclusion and to comply with it. In material ways, we can see that even if states have the sovereign right to control the movement of persons across their borders (Simmons 2001), this does not mean that they have the capacity to do so when the drivers making these borders permeable are simply too strong. If domestic relocation does not bring climate migrants to safety, states have material reasons for supporting a human right to relocate that includes the possibility for them to move abroad. By recognizing the climate migrants' claim and assuming their role as climate migrant receivers, states can protect themselves against having to face a new and much larger refugee crisis in the future. First, making the right to relocate a human right will set the duties for every signatory state to become a climate migrant receiver and this would mean that the "burden" would have, at least in principle, to be proportionally shared with other states. Second, rather than facing a massive uncontrolled influx of impoverished migrants through their borders and destabilizing their political, economic, and cultural systems, a human right to relocate that includes the possibility of resettlement abroad would enable relocations to be controlled and planned to happen before the complete impoverishment of the migrants. In such conditions, climate migrants would be less likely to strain the state's systems and more able to contribute to them, be it in terms of tax returns and of valuable cultural exchanges.

In non-material ways, accepting exceptions to the state's right to control their borders that arise in special circumstances is, from the international perspective, what justifies border control in the first place. In this sense, human rights can be said to emerge in order to regulate the exceptions and highlight the circumstances in which states are obliged to put their national agendas aside and act responsively as members of the international community. To do that is not necessarily a benevolent attitude, but a way of ensuring the just and peaceful functioning of the overall system. From that point of view, assigning states a responsibility to respond primarily to their members is a way of ensuring effectiveness, representation, and accountability. In other words, it is a way of ensuring the protection of a parcel of individuals that falls into a certain jurisdiction as a kind of division of labor defined by history. In normal circumstances, state 'A' responds to 'a' individuals and state 'B' to 'b' individuals in a way that 'b' individuals would be outsiders to the 'A' state and 'a' individuals would be outsiders to 'B' state. But human rights set a threshold where to be an insider or an outsider must not matter in terms of enjoying the basic conditions for a human life. If, for some reason, 'b' individuals are not able to meet these basic conditions and state 'A' refuses to extend them protection, from an international point of view, the very function of state borders ceases to be one of protecting a parcel of individuals to becoming one of preventing another parcel of individuals to enjoy protection—which is substantially different. In exceptional circumstances, shifting from the former function to the latter either revokes the justification for the state's sovereign right to control their borders because they do not accomplish the function they are meant to or it undermines the very idea of human rights and of the international sphere. This means that limiting the right to relocation to the domestic sphere by default, providing that we cannot guarantee that they will be able to reach a safe territory, would undercut the possibility of merging insiders and outsiders into humanity in a situation in which it is necessary — an ideal that underlines the very core of the notion of human rights. A human right to relocate irrespective of borders would then emerge as a way of giving centrality to the protection of the humanity of climate migrants and secure for them the possibility to resettle in a safe territory that would, otherwise, be regulated by individual states according to their own agendas.

Conclusion

Syrian men, who have traditionally extended families, are almost complete strangers to the city environment in Sivas. Some participants overly expressed that they want to have many wives and children and to establish an extended family. These cultural practices mentioned by the men in our study show the indispensable hegemonic compositions in the memory of Syrian men in general. None of these compositions highly exists in Sivas city environment, to which they migrated because of the war in Syria. Hence, social rules and habits that constitute all these social relations are highly weakened, unsustainable and unreliable now. The new social and professional relations that are built in this new environment lay the basis of 'non-places' for the immigrant men. These places melt away the identities of the older relations, upon which their relations and their histories based on genealogical lines had been built.

In these non-places, in this newly formed nuclear family environment, Syrian men attempt to regain the power, which forms the basis of the hegemonic masculinity, brought by the old cultural practices that they desire through 'patriarchal negotiations'. As mentioned by Certeau, men strive for turning non-places into the areas of 'strategy' that can be used against their wives, places in which they have the sense of belonging, places that have specific meanings for them. Against these strategic moves of men, women, as mentioned by Certeau, use 'tactics'. Women act in a way that they obtain relative autonomy and benefits. Women strive for creating more favourable moments and gain an advantage by using potential opportunities of daily life although they are assumed to be weaker and subordinate to men. They try to put some specific habits, attitudes and exercises into practice in this new environment that they feel out of place. For instance, completing their education, working at paid employment, getting out of the house with or without their husbands, wandering around shops, doing some shopping are some of these 'tactics'. Patriarchal negotiations are, in a sense, made of the complicated relations between these strategies and tactics.

Syrian men who migrated to Sivas try to regain the hegemonic position they once had in Syria, which reflects the male dominant structure that they desire. They strive to regain this position through their spouses in the new urban environment. Women, on the other hand, attempt to create fields in which they can experience individuality in this new urban environment.

Along with their efforts in this unfamiliar environment, Syrian men try to incorporate themselves into the power relations between local male residents in Sivas. They try to exhibit their existence in this world, which is dominated through strategies. For instance, business relationships are completely based on strategies, and Syrian men attempt to redefine their professional status. So, in the context of these strategic relations, actions of Syrian men may be perceived by others as tactics. Striving to have a say in the social order, to obtain a place, and to make more profit, are some of their aspirations in relation to the dominant power structure. In this context, it can be said that men enter a network of two-dimensional relations.

On the one hand, they try to sustain the in-house, male-dominant traditions that they were accustomed to, on the other hand, they try to accustom into the pragmatic relations of social environments that they recently met. These processes turn their subjective locations into more negotiable, relatively fragile positions. Syrian immigrant males try to integrate into the conditions of Turkey, to which they are strangers, by leaving behind the devastating war traumas.

Further, they want to synthesize previous hegemonic masculinity models on which they established their relationships for a long time, with the hegemonic masculinity models that they met in Turkey. They attempt to achieve this through their relations with spouses, but their endeavours are not always successful. The position of women has undergone a process of change along with the new conditions in the host country, and this change has enabled women to use some tactics in specific fields of life. This is the point that leads to patriarchal negotiations between men and women. Some Syrian women now have to work, to earn money which in turn enables them to have a say in male-female relationships. All these newly introduced factors increase their chance in negotiations with their husbands. This situation changed the perception of manhood on which Syrian men built their identities back in Syria.

As a result, although the concepts of war and migration didn't completely undermine male-dominant relations between Syrian men and women, they have caused a transformation in these relations in a new context and intention. This transformation has created new positions in power relations between men and women. Both Syrian men and women transform the places in their new environments, which are non-places for them since the day they arrived, into meaningful places through the use of different tactics and strategies.

Acknowledgments

This research is funded by the Globalizing Minority Rights Project (NRC 2016-2020/259017) and by Stadler Jacobsen's Research Fund (2018). For feedback on previous versions of this paper, I am grateful to J. Peixoto, A. Vitikainen, N. Khoury, A. K. Anderson, Y. Yuksekdag, N. Holtug, K. L.-Rasmussen, S. Lægaard, S. Parekh, M. Egan, T.I. Hanstad, and C. Heyward.

References

Bronen, R. and D. Pollock. Climate Change, Displacement and Community Relocation: Lessons from Alaska. May 2017. Norwegian Refugee Council (NRC) and the Alaska Institute for Justice (AIJ). Available at: https://www.nrc.no/globalassets/pdf/reports/nrc-alaska_relocation-screen.pdf

Carens, J. (2013). The Ethics of Immigration. Oxford University Press.

Forst R. (2012) The Justification of Human Rights and the Basic Right to Justification. A Reflexive Approach. In: Corradetti C. (eds) Philosophical Dimensions of Human Rights. Springer, Dordrecht.

Freeman, M. (2011). Human Rights: An Interdisciplinary Approach. 2nd edition. Polity Press.

Gemenne, F. (2017). "The Refugees of the Anthropocene". (B. Mayer & F. Crépeau, Eds.). In Research Handbook on Climate Change, Migration, and the Law. Edward Elgar Publishing.

Gibney, M. (2004). The Ethics and Politics of Asylum: Liberal Democracy and the Response to Refugees. Cambridge University Press.

Griffin, J. (2008). On Human Rights. Oxford University Press.

International Organization for Migration. (2011). Glossary on Migration. 2nd Edition. International Migration Law No. 25, IOM, Geneva, p. 33, available at http://publications.iom.int/bookstore/index.php?main_page=product_info&cPath=56&products_id=1380 [accessed 11 September 2018].

Kintisch, E. (2009). Projections of Climate Change go from bad to worse, scientists report. Science, Vol. 323, 20, pp. 1546-7.

Liao, M. (2009). Agency and Human Rights. Journal of Applied Philosophy, 27(1), 15-25. Retrieved September 11, 2018, from https://onlinelibrary.wiley.com/doi/abs/10.1111/j.1468-5930.2009.00470.x.

Neuteleers, S. (2011). Environmental Refugees: A Misleading Notion for a Genuine Problem. In Ethical Perspectives 18(2):229-48.

McAdam, J. (2017). Climate Change, Forced Migration, and International Law. Oxford University Press.

Miller, D. (2016). Is there a right to immigrate? (S. Fine & L. Ypi, Eds.). In Migration in Political Theory: The Ethics of Movement and Membership. Oxford University Press.

--. (2016b). Strangers in our Midst: The Political Philosophy of Immigration. Harvard University Press.

Nair, P., & United Nations University Institute on Globalisation. (2017, June 20). Refugee or migrant? Sometimes the line is blurred. Retrieved September 11, 2018, from https://theconversation.com/refugee-or-migrant-sometimes-the-line-is-blurred-79700

Nicholson, C. T. (2017). 'Climate-induced migration': Ways forward in the face of an intrinsically equivocal concept (B. Mayer & F. Crépeau, Eds.). In Research Handbook on Climate Change, Migration, and the Law. Edward Elgar Publishing.

Oliver-Smith, A. (2009). Nature, society, and population displacement: toward an understanding of environmental migration and social vulnerability. InterSecTions 'Interdisciplinary Security ConnecTions' Publication Series of UNU-EHS No. 8, Bonn.

Poncelet, A. (2009). Bangladesh Case Study Report: 'The Land of Mad Rivers' [Online: EACH-FOR Environmental Change and Forced Migration Scenarios].

Rancière, J. (2000). Le Partage du Sensible: Esthétique et Politique. Paris: La Fabrique Éditions.

Simmons, John A. (2001). "On the Territorial Rights of States". Philosophical Issues, 11: 300-26.

UN General Assembly, Convention on the Elimination of All Forms of Discrimination against Women, 18 December 1979, A/RES/34/180, available at: http://www.refworld.org/docid/3b00f2244.html [accessed 11 September 2018].

UN General Assembly, Convention on the Rights of Persons with Disabilities : resolution / adopted by the General Assembly, 24 January 2007, A/RES/61/106, available at: http://www.refworld.org/docid/45f973632.html [accessed 11 September 2018].

UN General Assembly, Convention on the Rights of the Child, 20 November 1989, United Nations, Treaty Series, vol. 1577, p. 3, available at: http://www.refworld.org/docid/3ae6b38f0.html [accessed 11 September 2018].

UN General Assembly, Convention Relating to the Status of Refugees, 28 July 1951, United Nations, Treaty Series, vol. 189, p. 137, available at: http://www.refworld.org/docid/3be01b964.html [accessed 11 September 2018].

UN General Assembly, Elimination of all forms of racial discrimination, 26 October 1966, A/RES/2142, available at: http://www.refworld.org/docid/3b00f1d734.html [accessed 11 September 2018].

UN General Assembly, Universal Declaration of Human Rights, 10 December 1948, 217 A (III), available at: http://www.refworld.org/docid/3ae6b3712c.html [accessed 11 September 2018].

The UN Refugee Agency, 06 Nov 2016, Displacement linked to climate change is not a future hypothetical – it is a current reality, available at : http://www.unhcr.org/news/latest/2016/11/581f52dc4/frequently-asked-questions-climate-change-disaster-displacement.html [accessed 24 September 2018].

CHAPTER 4

CLIMATE CHANGE MIGRATION AS AN ADAPTATION STRATEGY: THE ADAPTATION APPROACH THEORY AND THE PARIS AGREEMENT

Giulia Manccini Pinheiro

Introduction

In the 1990s scholars and experts predicted that climate change would trigger mass human mobility within the following decades (Geddes, Sommerville, 2013). However, climate change effects are often not the only cause of movement, as people also consider other factors such as economic situation, political stability, insecurity, attachment to a territory, the cost of relocation and their perspectives on a new place to settle (Mayer, 2011). At the same time, climate change effects can also exacerbate other social problems like population growth in dangerous areas, widespread poverty, famine and pandemic diseases (Myers, Kent, 1995).

Except in the case of a major environmental disaster, when immediate displacement is the only alternative, climate change plays a combined role with other causes of mobility. For this reason, the direct nexus between the climate change and the decision for move is often questioned, however, there is general acceptance that climate change has at least a partial role on the decision to move (Black, 2011, p.30). In this context, climate change migration is a complex issue that poses large challenges to national governments and international cooperation.

In this sense, this essay aims to investigate the Adaptation Approach theory and whether the Paris Agreement and the Intended Nationally Determinate Contribution fully reflect the theory. It will first consider the climate change migration phenomenon and its complexity, secondly it will analyze the Adaptation Approach theory developed by Mariya Gromilova in 2016[1] , as a way to face climate change migration challenges and lastly it will evaluate whether the Paris Agreement adopted this theory way of face the question or

---

[1] The theory was developed as part of Maryia Gromilova PhD thesis in 2015, but published on a journal in January 2016, before the Paris Agreement.

not.

Climate change migration phenomenon

Climate Change migration is a complex phenomenon. It can have different driving reasons besides the climate change effects, such as political instability, economic opportunities, social conflicts and even other environmental factors such as air pollution, soil contamination, lack of natural resources, deforestation, etc. Regarding the climate change role on migration, this essay adopts the KNOMADs (2013) study about the four paths by which climate change may affect migration, either directly or, more likely, in combination with other factors. The first are changes in weather patterns that contribute to longer-term drying trends that affect access and production of essential resources. The second are the rising sea-levels and glaciers melt that cause massive and repeated flooding and that render low-lying areas uninhabitable in the longer-term. The third are the increased frequency and magnitude of weather-related acute natural hazards that destroy infrastructure and livelihoods and requires people to relocate. And the last is the intensification of the competition over natural resources that may exacerbate pressures contributing to conflict.

The mobility can have distinct durations: the movement can be temporary, for instance, after a natural disaster when people can go back after the effects are finished; medium-duration, as it might take a longer time for the area to recover from the environmental issues; or permanent, in cases where the effects were so intense that recovery is impossible, and people cannot return to their habitats. Additionally, the extension of the mobility can also vary as the movement can be: internal, inside the country borders; regional, to the neighboring countries; or international, to more distant countries.

Regarding the motivation, the Internal Displacement Monitoring Centre (IDMC, 2015, p.16) defines 'displacement as the forced movement as it tends to emphasize pushing factors to leave and migration as a voluntary displacement as it emphasizes pull factors at the intended destination'. Nevertheless, the difference between voluntary and forced movement is particularly difficult to distinguish during slowly evolving disasters and the grey area between these two extremes is large and leave people in a vulnerable situation. Thus, since the definition between forced and volunteer is controversial, this study uses the word migration to cover all kinds of human movement, regardless of the motivation, duration or extension of the movement.

The multiplicity of causes and situations makes more difficult to define only one category or to develop specific scientific studies. Moreover, international law offers little help, since there are normative gaps under the forced mobility legislation which prevent most cases of climate change migrants from being considered under existing frameworks or for acquiring a defined legal status. The forced mobility existent protection is only for the people who fit the 1951

Geneva Convention and 1967 Additional Protocol's definition of refugee (Piguet, 2012), and it leaves out people displaced by conflicts, famine, pandemics, and disasters. These gaps also prevent the establishment of mechanisms for their protection (Biermann, Boas, 2008).

Whereas the studies about it started on the 90s, the impacts of climate change in internal and international migration was first worldwide recognized in 2010, when the Parties to the UN Framework Convention on Climate Change (UNFCCC) adopted the Cancun Adaptation Framework, which called on all countries to take 'measures to enhance understanding, coordination and cooperation with regard to climate change induced displacement, migration and planned relocation, where appropriate, at national, regional and international levels.' [UNFCCC, 2010, para.14(f)].

The Cancun Declaration is a non-binding instrument concluded within the UNFCCC framework, which nevertheless has implications that go far beyond a single declaration of intentions. It placed climate change migration firmly on the climate change adaptation agenda and established the dominant language to be used in advocacy works (Nash, 2017). The language factor is extremely important, because there is a large controversy over the term to reference it. As showed above, the movements can vary in many ways and choosing one term to represent this diverse category is a challenge, since each term has deep implications of legal framework and political background. Paragraph 14(f) of the Cancun agreement defined three types of movements: climate change induced displacement, migration and planned relocation. The International Organization for Migration (IOM), in this context, drew a broader definition of migration as "[t]he movement of a person or a group of persons, either across an international border, or within a State. It is a population movement, encompassing any kind of movement of people, whatever its length, composition and causes; it includes migration of refugees, displaced persons, economic migrants, and persons moving for other purposes, including family reunification" (IOM, 2014).

According to this definition, migration no longer refers only to voluntary movements, as stated by the IDMC, but also encompasses forced movements that are separated out in the Cancun formulation. In this context, this essay uses the term "climate change migration" and "climate change human mobility" as synonyms to refer to all the different types of human movement related to climate change, including internal and cross border movement, as discussed above, unless specified in another way – as in the Paris Agreement.

The next session will analyze the Adaptation Approach theory developed by Gromilova as a proposal to address climate change migration.

Adaptation Approach Theory

The adaptation approach to environmental change migration is defined, according to Gromilova (2016), as a proactive approach in which migration, induced displacement and planned relocation are used as adaptation measures that allow people to adjust to climate change by moving from places at risk.

The theory proposes the use of the established Human Rights Law and the United Nations Framework Convention on Climate Change (UNFCCC) rules and principles to impulse international cooperation and its mechanisms (mainly the NAPs and NAPAs and the founding systems) to place migration as an adaptation measure that is entitled to use the funds and support system for adaptation.

The main difference of this theory and the reason it was chosen for this paper is the placement of migration not only as an issue to address after it happened, but also as a preventive measure that valorizes human dignity. Moreover, the theory does not propose one answer to all the climate change mobilities, it rather emphasizes the difference of movement according to the regions and situations, giving margin to countries to develop their strategies. Therefore, instead of one solution to all different kind of movements, the theory establishes the minimum standards and principles for action and international cooperation, but it lastly places the policy solution in the countries' hands. This session will briefly analyze the theory main features.

Human Rights Law

The theory proposes the use of recognized *erga omnes* Human Rights law for determining the minimum standards that would entitle a person or a community to an adaptation strategy. The identification of these human rights was already done by the Human-Rights-based approach, but for different purposes.

McAdam investigated the human rights framework for finding what rights entitle the application of the *non-refoulement* principle[2]. Through her research, she finds out that the right to life[3] and the right not to be subject to torture inhuman or cruel treatment, if violated, can trigger the non-refoulement principle. In this context, if a person might have these rights violated if sent back to their country, they have the right not to be sent back, according customary international law and jurisprudence.

However, despite presenting an innovative view, it is unlikely that courts will accept the climate change as the actor which is responsible for violating human rights. The possibility of human rights violation entitling the *non-refoulement* principle can be found in "very exceptional" cases and any of them related to

---

[2] According to the principle of non-refoulement, asylum seekers already present within a jurisdiction cannot be removed by that state to a country where the person will face a real risk of persecution or exposure to torture, inhuman treatment or other serious human rights violations. UNHCR, UNHCR Note on the Principle of Non-Refoulement, November 1997. Available at <http://www.refworld.org/docid/438c6d972.html>. Accessed on 20 November 2017.

[3] "The right to life is very closely connected to other human rights. The right to an adequate standard of living under human rights law, including adequate food, clothing, housing and the continuous improvement of living conditions, and the right not to be deprived of means of subsistence, have been argued to be as necessary components of the right to life, which are compromised where global warming leads to the destruction of people's ability to hunt, fish, gather, or undertake subsistence farming". MCADAM, 2011, p.20.

climate change migration so far. It also only focuses on one person pledge on Court, while it was seen before that climate change migration might affect entire communities.

For these reasons, Gromilova only uses the rights identified by the referred approach as minimum standards of guarantee, that if in danger to be violated, would entitle the community to an adaptation plan involving resettlement or relocation.

International Climate-Change Law

Climate-Change is the trigger of all the environmental change phenomena described by KNOMAD's study. So, the theory extracts the obligations arising from the United Nations Framework Convention on Climate Change (UNFCCC) principles and uses the mechanisms offered by this framework for developing the Adaptation Strategies. The theory identifies only the principles that are accepted as customary international law and place them as obligations.

In the context of climate-change migration, it can be claimed that states did not respected the non-harm principle because their GHG emissions caused damage to other countries. However, only in the broaden sense since it is hard to find a direct link of one state emission to other state specific damage.

The Precautionary Principle is the answer of all the questioning related to the scientific certainty of the nexus between displacement and climate change. Since it declares that there is no need to wait for harm and even when climate change was not the only cause of migration, it is necessary to take a precautionary approach. Despite the disagreement on the number of affected people, it is a fact that migration due to climate change is inevitable (Graeme, Bedford, 2011). This principle is essential to the development of the adaptive approach because it can mobilize adaptation efforts before the complete harm or disaster happens, as it requires assistance for adaptation instead of help for an after-harm.

Lastly, the *Principle of Common but Differentiated Responsibilities* impulses international cooperation in developing adaptive strategies and founding the strategies in other affected countries because of the common responsibility for combating climate change and its adverse effects.

Human migration due to climate change varies according to the region and the environment around them. Consequently, the adaptation strategy should be developed according to the land and region's characteristics where it takes place. The UNFCCC has provisions for states to develop adaptation measures for climate change and its consequences. One of the central tools is the National Adaptation Programs of Actions and the National Adaptation Plans that enables Parties to formulate plans as a means of identifying medium and long term adaptation needs and developing and implementing strategies and programmes to address those needs.

Since Article 14(f) from the Cancun Declaration recognized that migration, displacement and planned relocation are strategies of adaptation for climate-change and invited all Parties to cooperate regarding specific actions on national, regional and international levels, the Adaptation Approach theory concludes that these strategies can become part of National Adaptation Plans. In this context, countries can identify the kind of dangers its population faces and design a more coherent and comprehensive process of adaptation. Concerning the financial resources, the theory determines that once migration is recognized as an adaptation strategy, the UNFCCC provides four main funds for adaptation: The Least Develop Countries Fund, the Adaptation Fund, the Special Climate Change Fund, and the Green Climate Fund.

Paris Agreement

The Paris Agreement was reached on the 21st Conference of the Parties in 15 December 2015. Briefly, its structure includes the establishment of its main goals in Article 2 and the setting of three main action areas: mitigation (Articles 3-6), adaptation (Article 7) and loss and damage (Article 8). However, the first two have a larger weight than the last one, that can be interpreted as confined within narrow bounds (Viñuales, 2015).

The action areas need to be addressed in the national commitments. In this context, the countries were invited in 2013 during the Warsaw Conference to prepare and submit Intended Nationally Determined Contributions (INDCs) in 2015, reflecting their voluntary national commitments to achieve global climate objectives on tackling climate change and reducing CO_2 emissions. The strategy was to adopt a bottom-up approach as the starting point to engage more countries in the process. However, there was a general understanding that these first contributions would need to be accompanied by information sufficient to generate clarity about the nature, type and stringency of the contributions (Rajamani, 2015).

Under the COP 21 Paris Agreement, adopted in December 2015, submitted INDCs automatically become Nationally Determined Contributions (NDCs) upon ratification of the Agreement, unless the State decided to submit a new NDC at the time of ratification.

Climate Change Migration in the Agreement

The Paris Agreement has formally included reference to migration on the Preamble 'Acknowledging that climate change is a common concern of humankind, Parties should, when taking action to address climate change, respect, promote and consider their respective obligations on (…) migrants (…)'. Despite not being legally binding, this mention was taken as a positive achievement of inserting migration into the COP decision (Nash, 2017). It did not, however, recognize the direct link of climate change causing people to migrate, but rather that there is a connection between these two issues, which is a first positive step, but it might not be enough to impulse countries to do something about it.

The other part relating human mobility and climate change is paragraph 50 of the Decision 1/CP.21, that requested the Executive Committee of the Warsaw International Mechanism for Loss and Damage to create a task force to develop recommendations on 'integrated approaches to avert, minimize and address displacement related to the adverse impacts of climate change'. Differently than the preamble, this provision does recognize that there is displacement caused by climate change impacts.

Considering the INDCs, from 162 submissions to the UNFCCC before COP 21, 33 submissions refers to migration in one of its different forms (IOM, 2017). It is important to note that among these countries, 46% are from Africa, 33% from Asia-Pacific and Oceania and 21% from Latin America, that are the regions most affected by climate change and the ones that have the largest climate migration flows.

The IOM study on this question interpreted the references in a broaden way and separated them on three dimensions: (1) managing effects of climate change on security and the need to tackle and prevent adverse mobility effects such as the displacement of people due to natural disasters or migratory movements linked to climate change as push factor; (2) using migration as a possible adaptation strategy to climate changes through policy measures such as resettlement and relocation; (3) leveraging remittances and financial transfers from migrants and diasporas to contribute to climate action.

Regarding these references, some conclusions can be reached. Analyzing the language used, the word 'migrants' on the Preamble refers only to the countries obligations towards migrants in general and not necessarily climate change migrants. On the other hand, when referring to human mobility caused by climate change on the Decision 1/CP.21, the word choice was 'displacement', what invokes the forced movement post-disaster or post-factum and not the preventive measure.

Concerning the position of the topic on the Agreement, it only appears in Article 50, that is related with the loss and damage mechanisms. However, in practice, the climate-change related displacement should not only be connected with compensation for the people who has already been displaced (loss and damage mechanism) but also with preventive measures and long-term strategies to avoid more displacement or to reallocate safely an endangered community (adaptation measures). This is not only a formal problem, but a practical one, because the Agreement only predicts 'financial resources to assist developing country Parties with respect to both mitigation and adaptation', Article 9 (1), but not to loss and damage mechanism.

In this context, the mention to displacement caused by climate change effects is the first recognition of the issue on a binding instrument, what represents a victory for advocacy groups and extremely vulnerable countries. On the other hand, the word choice and placement on the Agreement still represent the view that it is an issue to be addressed after it happened, to compensate people who has already been displaced.

Is the Adaptation Approach reflected by the Paris Agreement?

As mentioned above, the Paris Agreement mentions on climate change migration places it as an issue to be addressed and compensated, rather than a proactive adaptation strategy. The most serious implication of it is the absence of preventive measures to guarantee safety to the vulnerable communities and the lack of access to Adaptation Funds and other financial resources. In this context, the Parties general agreement does not reflect the Adaptation Approach theory. However, a further analysis can demonstrate some incorporation of the theory.

Viñuales (2015, p.7) defends that a broaden interpretation of Article 7 provisions on adaptation can be done to incorporate climate-change migration. According to the author, Article 7 (5) calls from appropriate consideration of *'vulnerable group communities and ecosystems'* and for *'integrating adaptation into relevant socioeconomic and environmental policies and actions'*. Additionally, the resilience and vulnerability reduction sought through adaptation plans encompasses responses to extreme weather events and slow onset events, that can be the relocation of communities vulnerable to them.

This position seems to be adopted by the most affected countries, because from the 33 INDCs related to migration, 23 belong to 2nd IOM category related to the use of migration as a possible adaptation strategy to climate changes through policy measures such as resettlement and relocation. This demonstrates that some countries are willing to view migration as an adaptive measure rather than a forced last choice action. Preventive measures of resettlement and relocation guarantee that the mobility is made in a safer way and considers human dignity.

It also enforces the idea that climate change migration is a complex phenomenon that does not have a single solution, but the focus needs to be on the national strategy. Unfortunately, this does not guarantee that these countries will have access to financial resources and other forms of international cooperation related to adaptation to put in action their plans.

Conclusion

The Adaptation Approach theory is interesting because it places migration as an adaptation measure under the UNFCCC framework, that at the same time places the countries in the main role to develop adequate regional strategies and foster international funding and cooperation. This approach considers the complexity of the climate change migration and does not intend to find a single solution. Moreover, it represents an innovative view because it focuses on proactive measures, in a way that the human mobility is made in a more planned and dignified way than waiting for the worse to impulse migration.

The Paris Agreement can be seen as a first step towards a common goal and its references to climate change related migration is a reason to be positive about the countries awareness of the issue. Nevertheless, the Agreement still places migration as a reactive measure in the loss and damage action, instead of an adaptation measure. This means that the Adaptation Approach was not formally incorporated in the Paris Agreement.

However, some provisions concerning adaptation can be interpreted in a broaden way to include social actions such as migration and relocation. Moreover, most of the INDCs that includes certain kind of human mobility refers to it as an adaptation measure, what reinforces the idea that the strategy needs to be adopted in a national context firstly. It is necessary the ratification of INDCs and its developments to further analyze if international cooperation and funding will be applicable to human mobility strategies.

References

Biermann, F, and I Boas. 2008. "Protecting Climate Refugees: The Case for a Global Protocol." Environment: Science and Policy for Sustainable Development.

Black, R. 2011. "Migration and Global Environmental Change: Future Challenges and Opportunities." UK Governement Office for Science.

Geddes, A, and W Sommerville. 2013. "Migration and Environmental Change: Assessing the Developing European Approach." Migration Police Institute Europe.

Gemenne, F, and J Blocher. 2017. "How Can Migration Serve Adaptation to Climate Change? Challenges to Fleshing out a Policy Deal." The Geographical Journal, 2017.

Gemenne, F, P Brücker, and D Ionesco. 2014. The State of Environmental Migration. SciencePo Press.

IOM. n.d. Migration, Climate Change and the Environment: IOM Perspective. Accessed May 4, 2019. https://www.iom.int/complex-nexus.

KNOMAD. 2015. "Environmental Change and Migration: State of the Evidence." Global Knowledge Platform on Migration and Development.

Mayer, B. 2011. "The International Legal Challenges of Climate-Induced Migration: Proposal for an International Legal Framework." Colorado Journal of International Environmental Law and Policy, 357–416.

Myers, N, and J Kent. 1995. "Environmental Exodus: An Emergent Crisis in the Global Arena." Climate Institute, 1995.

Nash, s. 2017. "From Cancul to Paris: An Era of Policy Making on Climate Change and Migration." Global Policy.

Piguet, E. 2012. "From 'Primitive Migration' to 'Climate Refugees': The Curious Fate of the Natural Environment in Migration Studies." In Annals of the Association of American Geographers, 148–62. Routledge.

UNFCCC. 2010. "Report of the Conference of the Parties on Its Sixteenth Session." Cancun: United Nations.

———. 2015. Adoption of the Paris Agreement. Decision CP.21.

Viñuales, J; E. 2015. "The Paris Climate Agreement: An Initial Examination." EENRG Working Papers, December.

CHAPTER 5

WHOSE DIASPORA? RETHINKING DIASPORA POLITICS: CHINA'S OVERSEAS CHINESE ENGAGEMENT IN TRANSNATIONAL SPACES

Carsten Schäfer

Introduction

In recent years, migration studies have increasingly started to draw attention to diaspora[1] strategies pursued by nation states. Indeed, diaspora policies are becoming a common phenomenon in the globalized world: Large sending states such as China long have developed policies intended to embrace and control "their diaspora". Using the example of Chinese migrants[2] in Austria, this article focusses on China's policies towards overseas Chinese and the complex transnational environments in which they unfold and evolve: How are these policies put into practice? And what actors exert influence on these processes? The mixed-method approach of this study is based on a qualitative content analysis of two Chinese language weeklies in Austria (*Europe Weekly*, hereafter: EW, and the *Huaxinbao*, HXB), of the Austrian Chinese internet forums www.achina.at (AC) and www.outuo.net (OT), as well as of Chinese state media. Included into the analysis are articles and postings that focus on activities of overseas Chinese organizations (mainly in Austria), on meetings between Chinese migrants and Chinese state officials, as well as on China's overseas Chinese strategies. In addition, the analysis includes a critical interpretation and analysis of official Chinese documents, official statements by Chinese politicians, teaching materials for Chinese cadres, official publications on China's diaspora politics, as well as of Chinese language research conducted in China.

The paper proceeds as follows: first, I look at China's official overseas Chinese discourse and the political apparatus that deals with overseas Chinese. According to Beijing, *all* overseas Chinese belong to China – regardless of their

---

[1] The term follows Brubaker's definition of "diaspora"; accordingly the paper "think[s] of diaspora not in substantialist terms as a bounded entity, but rather as an idiom, a stance, a claim" (2005, 12).

[2] In the context of this paper the terms overseas Chinese / Chinese migrants are based on an ethnic definition and refer to both Chinese citizens living abroad and to foreign passport holders of Chinese origin.

citizenship (Barabantseva, 2005). As a consequence, the last three decades have seen a continuous proliferation of state institutions and policies designed to harness the economic and political resources of overseas Chinese. Afterwards, the paper analyses the mechanisms for incorporating overseas Chinese into the Chinese state and for claiming the identity of "the sons and daughters of the Chinese nation" (China Internet Information Center, 2017). Large parts of the existing literature on China's diaspora politics exclusively focus on this state centered perspective, understanding Beijing's politics as an attempt to expand its power beyond territorial borders. Elena Barabantseva (2005) and James To (2012), for example, have examined how China seeks to embrace overseas Chinese and how the country extends the state's monopoly of power to Chinese residing outside of its borders. In that line, Pal Nyiri has stated that „we are likely to see […] relations between the PRC [People's Republic of China] and the overseas Chinese that might turn overseas Chinese organizations and businesses into representatives of PRC interests" (Nyiri, 1999, p.272). This state centered perspective is also prevalent in the literature on other sending state's diaspora strategies (Gamlen, 2006; Ho, 2011; Fransen & Siegel, 2011; Ragazzi, 2014; Adamson, 2015; Gazsó, 2017). In a way, all these approaches fall into the trap of methodological nationalism, and thus fail to account for the complex relations between state and non-state actors and between top-down and bottom-up forces in shaping diaspora politics. In sharp contrast to this, post-modern perspectives declare such nation state perspectives impractical when analyzing the dynamics of modern migration (West, 2014, p.94). Accordingly, the majority of literature by these "transnationalists" champion the idea that state institutions have (or soon will) become insignificant and irrelevant, losing control of migration processes. This in turn has, as some authors critically pointed out, "led to an overuse of concepts" (Schunck, 2014) such as transnationalism, which "often results in unwarranted minimalization of nation states' capacities to direct and coordinate how transnational processes are shaped." (Chin & Smith, 2012, p.35f.).

Against the backdrop of these contrasting perspectives, this article aims at capturing the inter-relational power dynamics, contestations and negotiations between different actors that are critical in defining and implementing diaspora politics – without *ex ante* disregarding one of these actors. The article hopes to broaden the theoretical focus on diaspora politics by not only paying attention to state regimes that enforce a specific kind of behavior by emigrants but by applying attention also to migrants as actors in their own right who challenge those regimes. By taking the example of the Tibet unrest 2008 the final part of the paper therefore addresses the question of how China's politics to instrumentalise overseas Chinese are exploited and re-shaped by overseas Chinese grassroots actors located in Austria.[3]

---

[3] The history of the Chinese in Austria is rather short. Numbers of Chinese immigrants started to rise only after the beginning of China's reform and opening policy in 1978, numbering from about 800 in the beginning of the 1980s to approximately 40,000 persons today. In this sense, the Austrian perspective can be regarded

Against this backdrop, the goal of this study is twofold: First, by shedding a light on the multiple actors involved in shaping diaspora policies, the paper calls for a theoretical reconceptualization of diaspora engagement politics. Based on my case study I present an analytical framework in which the state is no longer treated as the only unit of analysis but embedded in power relations encompassing multiple actors in national and transnational arenas. In order to understand diaspora policies, I argue that future research has to systematically engage with different influential factors that emanate from multiple diaspora, receiving country and sending states actors. In this spirit, the paper will hopefully contribute to the development of a more profound and comprehensive theory on diaspora engagement politics. Second, by way of relating China's diaspora policies to comparable politics of other states, I aim to fill the gap between the so far isolated sinologist studies and the growing field of diaspora politics studies, thus bringing together both sides and enriching data sets for future comparative analyses.

CHINA'S OVERSEAS CHINESE DISCOURSE AND DIASPORA APPARATUS

In official China, the approximately 60 million overseas Chinese are represented as constitutive elements of the Chinese nation. In this regard, the official notion of "overseas Chinese" includes both Chinese passport holders living abroad and ethnic Chinese with foreign citizenship (Barabantseva, 2005). While juridical differentiating between Chinese passport holders (huaqiao) and ethnic Chinese foreigners (huaren), Beijing's diaspora politics are – as noted in a textbook for cadres – directed "not only towards Chinese citizens, but also towards ethnic Chinese with foreign passports" (qiaowu gongzuo duixiang shi huaqiao, waiji huaren) (Qiaoban, 2006, p.2). Accordingly, both classifications are not only interchanged frequently or merged into one word – huaqiaohuaren; the unitary notion is also manifested in frequently used expressions such as "descendants of the Fiery Emperors and the Yellow Emperor" (yanhuang zisun), or "offspring of China" (huaxia zisun) (EW, 2014a) to address overseas Chinese. In line with this, China's president Xi Jinping had pointed out that overseas Chinese affiliations to China are based on "bloodline affection" (xueyuan qinqing) (Xi, 2017). Overseas Chinese are thus regarded as a part of the "big family of the Chinese nation" (zhonghua da jiating) (Zhongguo Qiaowang, 2014) grouped around the Chinese Communist Party (CCP) and bound to China by ties of blood, lineage, and culture (Nyiri, 2001): There is, in other words, a deep-rooted assumption that overseas Chinese „not only maintain their identity but also feel proud of being Chinese" (Shen, 2006, p.220) – and thus belong to China and not to their country of residence, regardless of their citizenship.

Such essentialist identity narratives are strongly interconnected to the

---

as a representative case study on China's diaspora engagement that started in 1978 and is mainly targeted on these "new migrants".

country's policy of "reform and opening up" that started in 1978. By embracing its "most precious resource" (zui baogui de ziyuan) (EW, 2014a), Beijing seeks to accumulate capital, import know-how and technology and foster it's international image (Qiu, 2011) and thus to enhance the countries global competitiveness. Therefore, in accordance with the government discourse China has created a corresponding political bureaucracy aimed at dealing with overseas Chinese matters. China's overseas Chinese policy is basically conducted and coordinated by the Overseas Chinese Affairs Office (OCAO), an administrative office under the State Council – the highest administrative authority in China – that was installed in 1978. The OCAO is responsible for researching the diaspora and providing base for the development of a diaspora strategy; its overall goal is "the coordination of policy formulations […], as well as monitoring their implementation" (Liu & van Dongen 2016, p.809). Besides the OCAO, Beijing has established a large number of institutions that are aimed at managing relationships with Chinese overseas (Barabantseva, 2005) – including the All-China Federation of Returned Overseas Chinese (ACFROC), the Chinese Civic Centers, or Chinese embassies around the globe, to only name a few. The shared objective of these institutions is to establish direct links with the overseas Chinese and to exercise influence and authority over them. Taken together, this apparatus of diaspora engagement politics equip Beijing with the capacity of political maneuvers within Chinese emigrant communities around the globe: Its political bodies are dedicated to bolster the image of China, to produce a communal mentality and sense of belonging amongst Chinese abroad, to monitor overseas Chinese and to define and exploit their soft power, financial and intellectual potentials.

Political measures: The case of Austria

The Chinese government has adopted a broad range of policies and programs targeting Chinese abroad. In order to obtain the loyalty and commitment of Chinese in Austria, to claim obligations from them and to propagate policy guidelines, Beijing has created numerous cultural, legal, social and political links between the Chinese state and the Austrian Chinese community. Especially overseas Chinese associations, language schools and media are used as "matchmakers" that function as points of contact and facilitate regular interactions with Chinese officials (Nyiri, 2007, p.120). Accordingly, in Austria, most newly founded overseas Chinese organizations in the last ten years were established with support or under supervision of Chinese authorities, including the China Councils for Promoting Peaceful Reunification, the Chinese Students Association or the Association for Promoting Scientific Cooperation (Schäfer, 2018). Furthermore, starting in 2006, Chinese authorities have begun to foster cooperation between Chinese state media and overseas Chinese media. As a result, both former independent Chinese language weeklies in Austria – the Europe Weekly and the Huaxinbao – are today to a large part produced in China by official mouthpieces of the CCP – which, unsurprisingly, brings about an increasingly homogeneous Chinese language media sphere in

Austria. In addition, China supports cooperation between state institutions and Chinese migrants' language schools in Austria in order to exert influence on their education programs (Thuno, 2001) and to strengthen Chinese roots and patriotism among Austrian born "Chinese" (EW, 2009). In 2015, all seven Chinese language schools in Austria targeting second generation Chinese were connected to the Chinese state bureaucracy.

The short outline illustrates the growing infrastructure connecting Chinese state authorities and overseas Chinese in Austria. China uses this structure for a continuous and extensive propaganda work and to disseminate nationalistic messages. In this context, the main efforts of developing relationships with the diaspora are pursued under the guiding theme of "going out and inviting in" (zou chuqu, qing jinlai) (Thuno, 2001; Barabantseva, 2005; To, 2012). Correspondingly, China frequently sends out official delegations to meet with Chinese migrants in Austria. From June 2011 to October 2013, Chinese authorities made at least 14 visits to Vienna (seven by the OCAO alone), resulting in relations with 30 out of 55 overseas Chinese associations, language schools and media outlets. Furthermore, the Chinese embassy keeps in touch with Chinese organizations in Austria by frequently holding gala dinners in celebration of welcoming new embassy personal, by observing emigrant association events or by organizing national celebrations and cultural events within the Chinese community – such as official anniversary celebrations remembering China's victory in the Sino-Japanese War (AC, 2010b) or traditional holidays such as the Spring Festival (EW, 2011b). In addition, Chinese authorities time and again organize "conferences" that bring together Chinese state authorities and Chinese overseas to propagate official government standpoints about a wide range of political topics. In a conference on the Tibet question (AC, 2012a) a delegation of "Tibet experts" from China for example claimed that "since ancient times Tibet is an inseparable part of China" (Xizang zigu shi zhongguo lingtu bu ke fenhai de yi bufen) and was "peacefully liberated" (heping jiefang) by the Communist Party in 1950, resulting in the "happy" (xingfu) place it is today. Other conferences correlate with political mega events in China such as the National People's Congress (EW, 2014b) or the 19th National Congress of the CCP (Qingtian Wang, 2018). Sometimes, gatherings are even used to denounce "the hypocrisy of Western democracy" (xifang minzhu de xuweixing) (AC, 2011a) or to eulogize "the correctness, suitability, and superiority of the Chinese democracy" (AC, 2013c).

China uses such meetings to actively claim "its" diaspora by disseminating essentialist identities that aim at bolstering nationalistic ties between Chinese inside and outside the PRC. In this line, participants frequently emphasize the migrants' obligation to uphold their "patriotic spirit" (aiguozhuyi jingshen) (Xinhua, 2013), their "love for the country" (aiguo) and their "pride in their nation" (minzu zihaogan) (AC, 2012b). By the same token, diaspora identities are reinforced by slogans according to which "Chinese cultural roots cannot be cut off" (zhonghua wenhua gen duanbuliao) (Renmin Ribao, 2008).

Schäfer

Furthermore, authorities use such gatherings to export official ideology and to assign certain expectations to overseas Chinese – even if such expectations about supporting China's national interests usually remain quite unspecific in nature and revolve around constantly recurring paroles. Speeches for example call upon overseas Chinese "to return to the homeland and contribute to China's economic upswing" (hui dao zuguo […] jingji jianshe zuochu nimen de gongxian) (EW, 2011a) or to "serving the country from abroad" (liu zai haiwai […] wei guo fuwu) (Xinhua, 2013), to act as "unofficial ambassadors" (minjian dashi), to propagate Chinese culture in the world (Qingtian Wang, 2018), to contribute to the "great rejuvenation of the Chinese nation", and to "safeguard China's national unity" (Western Returned Scholars Association 2018; EW 2011a) – or simply "to follow Chairman Xi" (xianying xi zhuxi; AC, 2013b).

Apart from the "going out"-strategy, Chinese authorities frequently sponsor travels to China for Austrian Chinese organizations with the very same efforts as described above, e. g. to contribute to China's modernization, to spur patriotism, and to enhance the understanding between China and other countries. During the last years, Austrian Chinese were received by the OCAO and the ACFROC (EW, 2011d) or attended the National Day in Beijing (EW, 2011b) and, as nonvoting delegates, the Chinese People's Political Consultative Conference (AC, 2013c). Additionally, Austrian born Chinese are frequently invited to participate in so called root-seeking summer camps that work to "bolster ethnic ties to home localities and to Chinese culture" (Thuno, 2001, p.924). At the same time, Chinese authorities are busy to create a legal framework that offers special treatment for overseas Chinese – such as tax benefits or the permission to purchase land in China (Barabantseva, 2005) –, in order to attract remittances, donations and foreign direct investments (Bolt, 1996) and to produce goodwill relationships with its diaspora in ideological and political terms. Especially in order to get hold of the estimated 4 million highly educated ethnic Chinese abroad (Wang 2017), China has recently introduced a multiple-entry visa that allows ethnic Chinese with foreign citizenship to stay in China for up to five years, "to streamline the process for overseas Chinese to 'return home' and to make it easy for them to visit families, conduct business and cultural exchanges and run personal errands in China" (China Daily, 2018).

Strategies for diaspora mobilization also include the frequent organization of large-scale and high profile global conventions which bring together people of Chinese origin from around the globe under the banner of the CCP. The 7th Forum on the Global Chinese Media for example was held in Qingdao on September 2013 and was attended by 450 overseas representatives from 58 countries – including members of the Austrian Europe Weekly – and by 150 Chinese state officials and state media operators (EW, 2011c). At the meeting, Chinese authorities broadcasted their propaganda messages and ascribed the role of "good voices of China", e. g. of pro-China lobbyists in their countries of residence, to overseas Chinese media. During the 7th Conference for Friendship of Overseas Chinese Associations in Beijing, which brought together 500 overseas Chinese from 119 countries (EW, 2014c), president Xi called upon ethnic Chinese to not forget their "Chinese blood" (zhonghua minzu xueye) and to make contributions "to the Chinese dream of national rejuvenation" (shixian zhonghua minzu da fuxing) (Zhongguo Qiaowang, 2014).

To sum up, China makes considerable efforts to turn overseas Chinese into a loyal force that represent its interests abroad. Incorporating overseas Chinese in symbolic, bureaucratic, and legal terms has become an essential part of China's modernity project. As a result, the political geography of China – including national narratives, the political apparatus, principles of belonging and the concept of border – has reshaped tremendously. Such politics not only blur the traditional divide between domestic politics and foreign policy, but also re-conceptualize the notion of the Chinese state: By reaching outside its national territory and thus challenging territorial and place-based definitions of sovereignty and citizenship, the CCP aims at extending the monopoly of power of the state to subjects located not only outside its territorial borders, but also outside its jurisdiction.

These politics have contributed to the image of overseas Chinese as a "fifth column" of the PRC that always "maintain its love towards the motherland" – as Germany's Manager Magazin had put it (Hirn, 2012). In the same token, James To (2014, p.280) has called overseas Chinese a "highly coordinated ethno-nationalist force with transnational loyalties", which "serve as a [...] ready supply of soft power to advance or support Beijing's outreach throughout the world." Going even further, the Australian author Clive Hamilton (2018) claimed in his book Silent Invasion that Chinese migrants would secretly support the PRC in taking over Australia. Such notions refer to the long-standing myth of an "overseas Chinese exceptionalism", according to which overseas Chinese never assimilate into their host country, but always "feel a powerful sense of attachment to the homeland" (Martin, 2012, p.331). And indeed, it has often pointed out that in economic terms, overseas Chinese contributions have significantly increased the capabilities of the Chinese state's modernization project in the last 40 years (Lin, 2000). Sometimes, overseas Chinese even publicly lobby on behalf of interests of the PRC. In Vienna, small groups of Chinese migrants for example have protested against a visit of the Dalai Lama to Vienna, or waved flags to welcome "their" president Hu Jintao on his state visit to Austria.

Yet, by taking a closer look at such state-diaspora-relations, we get a glimpse at the highly complex power relations between overseas Chinese grassroots movements and Chinese state politics that can hardly be grasped by such essentializing notions. The following case study about the Tibet unrest 2008 demonstrates that overseas Chinese, instead of simply "serving the country from abroad", sometimes turn out to be a double-edged sword for "their" home state and its political ambitions.

The Tibet unrest 2008: The spirits that I've cited my commands ignore

The 2008 Tibet unrest refers to Tibetan demonstrations and riots against Han-Chinese in China in March 2008, that soon were stamped down by the Chinese military. While politicians, human rights activists, the media and exile Tibetans in Austria and numerous other countries accused Beijing for its human rights violations and protested against Beijing's harsh handling of what was broadly perceived as righteous demonstrations against "the Chinese occupation of Tibet" (chinesische Besatzung Tibets) (Die Presse, 2008), China claimed that the riots were organized from abroad. The country not only asserted that "the Dalai Lama clique plotted and incited the Lhasa violence on March 14" (China Daily, 2008), but that „European and American forces" (Sun, Zhang & Li, 2014, p.192) had supported the separatists by "willfully distort[ing] Tibet's history and reality" and "groundlessly accus[ing]" China (ibid., 191), while in reality Tibetan people would live a "happy life" (People's Daily, 2008). Such narratives are well known in China and part of a nationalistic education that started in the early 1990s: „China's education system ensures that all students are well-aware of China's historical conflicts with ‚the West.' […] [A] common perception among Chinese citizens is that people from Western countries are prejudiced toward China and its citizens" (Hail, 2015, p.3). In March 2008, China thus called upon "1.3 billion Chinese people" inside and outside China to not allow any "person or force to undermine the stability of the [Tibetan] region" (People's Daily, 2008).

In March 2008, Chinese students in Austria made use of these narratives – yet they interpreted them in ways completely different to the Chinese government: A few days after riots had broken out in Tibet, Chinese students started to voice their anger against the "West" in their internet forum outuo.net. In a highly radicalized online environment, the majority of outuo users constantly berated Austrians as "pigs" (zhu) (OT, 2008g), "yellow colored dogs" (huangmao gou) (OT, 2008c) and "brainless" (naocan) (OT, 2008h) "enemies of China". Even more problematic, outuo users attacked Tibetans as "ungrateful" "barbarians" (yeman) (OT, 2008i), "bastards" (wangbadan) or "beggars" (qigai) (OT, 2008a). Some users even posted pictures of exile Tibetan club houses in Vienna and called for physical violence against Tibetans in the city (OT, 2008e). It is interesting to note that Chinese student's reactions in the United States were less hostile towards the host society (Yang, 2010). Thus it seems that the harsh anti-Austrian stances among many outuo users were not only influenced by state narratives they had learned since their childhood, but also by a constant feeling of discrimination at the hands of Austrians, which has been one of the recurring themes in the internet forum for years (see for example OT, 2010). Indeed, even the "2015 Report of the European Commission against Racism and Intolerance" has defined racism and xenophobia as severe problems in Austria. Anti-Austrian slander became even stronger after high ranking Austrian politicians turned up during exile Tibetan demonstrations in front of the Chinese embassy in Vienna and after the Austrian police had failed to hinder a Tibetan to climb up the facade of the Chinese embassy to steal the Chinese flag (OT, 2008d) – an incident that also aggravated the Han-chauvinistic online libel against Tibetans in Vienna who repeatedly – and often enthusiastically reported by Austrian media – called attention to themselves by way of several anti-China protests in the city.

Obviously, such online hate speech (especially with the Beijing Olympics ahead) not only sabotaged China's official image campaign depicting the country as a peaceful rising power, but also harshly counteracted official propaganda about a harmonious relation between Chinese and Tibetans in China. Thus not surprisingly, when the same students on March 22 used outuo.net as a platform to organize a demonstration in Vienna "to safeguard the motherland" (OT, 2008b), the Chinese embassy and the Chinese Students Association (that is associated with the embassy) stepped in and prohibited the demonstration (ibid.).

The students indeed caved in to the pressure by the embassy – yet at the same time turning their anger against the government body, accusing China's representatives of betraying Chinese interests (OT, 2008h). Since the CCP bases its legitimacy to a large extend on the historical claim of "liberating" China from foreign aggressors, any such questioning of the state's nationalist and patriotic stance is a highly dangerous attack on the CCP's claim to power (Hughes, 2000). In the course of the following weeks the tense situation between the radicalized students and the embassy further heated up when outuo users became aware that self-declared "patriotic" Chinese grassroots movements had started to mushroom up in numerous places around the globe and that Chinese in other countries were apparently free to take to the streets (OT, 2008f) – in some places even with the support of the local embassy (Nyriri, 2011). This phenomenon demonstrates that notions such as "the sending state" sometimes are too simple to grasp the complexity of diaspora engagement: different embassies – i. e. key state actors in China's overseas Chinese engagement – obviously took different approaches towards nationalistic overseas Chinese in different localities. In this instance, the Chinese state reached out to overseas Chinese through a multitude of actors that evidently lacked a centralized orchestration – which, in turn, further complicated the situation in Austria.

In a first attempt to regain control of the students in Vienna, the Students Association repeatedly intervened in the online discussions; in several postings it not only defended the embassy's attitude but also demonstratively labeled Tibetans as "fellow countrymen" and Austrians as "friends" (OT, 2008c) – yet without obtaining the desired result. Especially the latter aspect is interesting, since the notion of "Austrian friends" was not a part of the official anti-Western state propaganda, but rather an ad hoc reaction to the specific Austrian context. It was only after these attempts had failed that the embassy finally changed its strategy. After having suppressed a large scale demonstration for weeks, the embassy – or, to be more specific, the Chinese Students Association, an organization sponsored by and interlinked to the embassy – did a sudden U-turn and publicly announced a demonstration in Vienna on April 19. In a public call-up posted at outuo, the Chinese Students Association not only appealed to outuo users to participate in the demonstration, but it also – obviously still concerned about the student's Han-chauvinism – gave exact instructions in terms of slogans and topics, as well as in relation to the form and content of flyers and posters. Astonishingly, the Chinese Students Association even defined behavior rules for demonstrators, which included, among other things, a ban on speaking to Austrian media representatives (OT, 2008d).

The case study demonstrates the Chinese government's vulnerability at times when overseas Chinese make use of the very narratives ascribed to them: In a twist of irony the same institution that expended great effort to obstruct nationalistic outburst in the end had to go along with populist demands and even tried to become the spearhead of the nationalistic movement. The example of the Tibet unrest demonstrates that the display of patriotism and nationalism is not simply a manifestation of obedience to the diaspora state. In March 2008, Chinese migrants have not simply adopted identity categories ascribed to them by the Chinese nation state, but rather re-invented them according to the specific contexts they encountered in Austria (while at the same time believing to perform "patriotic" duties expected by their nation), thus creating identity narratives that excluded Chinese state institutions from the patriotic Chinese "we": The same nationalism that was constantly demanded from (overseas) Chinese by the Chinese state had suddenly turned against this very state.

While China seeks to harness overseas Chinese to "defend the country's core interests" (China Internet Information Center, 2017), the April 19 demonstration was, even if it seems to prove this case at first sight, quite the opposite: It rather endangered official Chinese interests. China's politics in Vienna were mainly driven by the goal of avoiding unwelcome diaspora activity in the international arena. Interesting is, of course, that China in the end had found a way to comply with "its" diaspora's demands and to even turn them into a profitable outcome. It might be exactly the before mentioned decentralised nature of the diaspora state that allowed for this high degree of flexibility – and for retaining parts of its power in the end.

Discussion

China – as many countries with a large diaspora – takes great efforts to embrace overseas Chinese and to claim their identity, mainly to pursue political and economic interests. Yet, in contrast to traditional state-centric approaches – as well as in contrast to stereotypes implying that overseas Chinese act as a "fifth column" for China –, this articles shows that the Chinese government so far has not succeeded in gaining unconditional acceptance by overseas Chinese. Cases such as the April 19 demonstration to a large degree dismantle the perception that overseas Chinese are the extension of the PRC. Especially the internet allows for expressing dissent and mobilization around common goals and thus to constitute a discursive power that re-tailors state narratives in accordance to own needs; such narratives in turn can exert great pressure on the very state that tries to embrace these emigrants. In such instances, Beijing has to realize it can neither monopolize definitions of (overseas) Chinese identities nor can it expect overseas Chinese to simply align with predefined expectations while barring them from shaping the agenda of diaspora politics. In contrast, the Chinese in Vienna proofed to be factor that can influence the outcomes of China's diaspora policy.

The case study thus demonstrates that national governments are not the only actors harnessing diasporas; on the contrary, "the diaspora" is a group open to engagement and mobilization by a multiple set of actors and for different agendas and interests. As long as overseas Chinese expectations can be satisfied by cooperation with China – such as in terms of economic activities targeting the huge Chinese market – overseas Chinese easily go along with China's aspirations; yet, when China counteracts on these expectations, overseas Chinese turn easily against the Chinese state.

One of the reasons for this not so closed relationship might be the lack of provisions offered by China to Chinese abroad – for example social and welfare services. In this sense, instead of simply replicating traditional citizen-sovereign relationships on the transnational level, China's policies basically come down to what Gamlen (2006, p.5) has called a "thin sovereignty": Gamlen (2006, p.13) argues that if states fail to extent civil and social rights to their diasporas while "expecting to leverage shared national identity in order to get something for nothing from emigrants, they are playing against the odds. [...] The strength of states' claims to legitimately extract benefits from 'their' diasporas arguably flows from their reciprocal provision of benefits". Yet China's constant claims about "putting people first and serving overseas Chinese [...] and safeguarding their interests" (China Internet Information Center, 2017) don't resonate much with reality: Users of the web forum outuo frequently express resentment towards the lack of activity and intervention by the Chinese state when they feel discriminated or otherwise in trouble (see for example OT, 2010 or OT, 2014). In this sense, China resembles what Gamlen (2006, p.19) has called an "exploitative state, which extract obligations without extending rights". Following the same logic, it seems that the institutional infrastructure implemented by China to manage overseas Chinese lacks the instruments to canalize feedback. Clashes about how to best assert "national interests" – such as during the Tibetan crisis – are the result. In a way, China's top down and paternalistic approach to its diaspora fits not with trans-national realities. In line with this, China's attempt to govern people that – in part – do not legally belong to China and that life beyond its territory proves to be quite difficult in practice. Looking at China's diaspora policy from this angle, it resembles a trial-and-error-approach that, apart from the formulation of basically guidelines, has not yet yielded in definite form and regulations. Indeed, by reaching out to its diaspora, China exposes itself to an environment coined by multiple state and non-state actors in a transnational arena, that China – due to the inability to simply transfer its monopoly of power to this fiercely contested arena – cannot control.

Towards A New Research Perspective

Both the importance and the merits of the existing literature on diaspora engagement politics are immense and indispensable. Yet, some problems remain, particularly in terms of state-centric perspectives predominant in most research. Ragazzi (2014, p.84) for example has argued "that the political-economical model of a state […] ultimately best explains the development of diaspora policies." This important aspect notwithstanding, sending state's institutions and policy formulations are no convincing indicators to measure the functionality of diaspora policies when seen isolated. Grassroots movements likewise are an independent variable in diaspora politics that need to be taken into consideration, since political and ideological struggles like those during the Tibet unrest would otherwise remain invisible to researchers. Migrants are independent actors with own motivations and agencies that wield power over state politics. This article demonstrates that such power relations, power struggles, negotiations and highly complex interactions between a large set of actors in multiple places have to be systematically taken into account when analyzing state politics, since they instantiate and characterize diaspora engagement practices.

Accordingly, the paper demonstrates the need to reassess and broaden the analytical framework in order to understand the design, implementation and outcome of diaspora politics. In this view, this article calls for a research perspective that draws attention to the processes in which the efforts of home states in reaching out to emigrants are re-defined by other actors. Without considering such power relations in the present case, it would have seem that overseas Chinese were simply orchestrated by the Chinese state – as some observers indeed have claimed (Thinley, 2008). Yet, by challenging state centrist approaches, we have to be careful to not throwing the baby out with the bath water and neglecting the state as a powerful actor completely. What, then, are the appropriate units of research? Drawing on the findings of this case study, we can identity the following set of actors that constitute diaspora politics:

- The Chinese party state and its various state institutions;
- Chinese migrants in Austria, whose actions and agendas where not only defined by diaspora politics, but at the same time by specific migration experiences shaped both by
  - the host state environment and
  - the actions and experiences of overseas Chinese groups outside Austria.

We can conclude from that, that China's diaspora politics are potentially shaped by influencing factors that emanate from an environment coined by four different ideal-typical social spaces, namely China, the country of residence, as well as local and transnational migrant groups. Combined, the four social spaces constitute a framework within which diaspora engagement is constructed and contested.

Obviously, these spaces should not be treated as fixed categories constituted by monolithic institutions; in contrast, a closer look reveals their internal distinctions and diversities – as could be seen in China's decentralized handling of the Tibet crisis. In this sense, the four spaces rather depict a trans-national and trans-local arena within which forces can be constituted that influence diaspora politics. Thus, these spaces are neither transfixed nor clearly market-off; they don't describe a static image of reality but define a potential set of actors – including institutions, organizations, political parties, networks, laws, media, or identity narratives – that, while permanently and context-dependent re-shaped and re-arranged, constantly aim at exerting influence on the lifeworld around them; in this way, boundaries between these spaces are constantly relocated, reinforced, pulled down and build up. In contrast to overly eclectic paradigms claiming that "everything is transnational" and neglecting the existence of a priori social structures, this concept not only keeps "the sending state" and "the diaspora" as potential influential factors inside the research perspective, but also incorporates (inadvertent) recipients of these politics into the analysis.

Researchers should neither ignore the influence of the state – as is often done by "transnationalists" – nor overemphasize it – as is done frequently by "state centrists". The relationship between transnationalism and nation states is not one of mutual exclusiveness; in contrast, both trends coexist in the globalized world. In this sense, the model proposed in this paper brings together post-modern paradigms and "pre-postmodern" perspectives, to a certain degree acknowledging the validity of both without generalizing either of them. Therewith, the analytical framework hopefully offers a more differentiated understanding of diaspora policies by looking at the logics, interests and mechanisms that drive both initiators and addressees of diaspora policies; in the same vein, it will hopefully contribute to the development of more solid theories on the matter.

The specifics of the new state-citizen-configurations brought about by diaspora politics in many aspects still remain quite unclear. This holds also true for the relation between the "national" and the "transnational". Chin and Smith (2012, p.31) have noted, that "transnational phenomena [often] are embedded in, unfold within, and/or are mediated through nation states". In the same line, transnational mobility not necessarily leads to cosmopolitism or multiculturalism but can contribute to hyper-nationalism. Diaspora politics force us to re-think concepts of society, citizenship, sovereignty, and territory. Some elements of these politics can be regarded as severe – and even hostile - incursions on host-states' territory, provoking tensions between sending and receiving states. Yet other elements generate win-win-situations for both sides, for example in terms of trade and development opportunities. Either way, China's case proves that diaspora politics have to be considered a growing force in world politics. We need to understand such politics – not only as scientists, but also as citizens of our states that should grasp both the chances and the risks implicated in them.

References

achina.at (2010a, undated). Zhu Aodili shiguan juxin bayi jianjun jie. Retrieved from www.achina.at/2010/aktiv/8.01.htm

achina.at (2010b, undated). Zhu Aodili shiguan juxing jinian kangzhan shengli 65 zhounian zuotanhui. Retrieved from www.achina.at/2010/aktiv/9.03.htm

achina.at (2012a, undated). Zhongguo Zangxuejia daibiaotuan fangao bing yu Ao qiaojie juxing Xizang de lishi yu wenhua zuotanhui. Retrieved from www.achina.at/2012/0616A/AA.htm

achina.at (2012b, undated). Hangzhoushi xia chengqu renmin zhengfu shangwu kaocha daibiaotuan fangwen Aodili. Retrieved from www.achina.at/2012/0623A/AA.htm

achina.at (2013a, undated). Diaoyudao wenti zhuuanti baogaohui. Retrieved from www.achina.at/2013/0417/2017.htm

achina.at (2013b, undated). 2013 nian Zhongguo meng Ouzhou gaofeng luntan zai Helan longzhong juban 2013. Retrieved from www.achina.at/2013/0704/2013.htm

achina.at (2013c, undated). Zhongguo de fazhan yu weilai – Aodili qiaojie zuotanhui. Retrieved from http://www.achina.at/2013/0419/2013.htm

Adamson, F. (2015). Blurring the Lines: Diaspora Politics and Globalized Constituencies. World Politics Review: Retrieved from http://www.worldpoliticsreview.com/articles/16224/blurring-thelines-diaspora-politics-and-globalized-constituencies

Ancien, D., Boyle M. & Kitchin, R. (2009). Exploring Diaspora Strategies: An International Comparison. Workshop report.

Barabantseva, E. (2005). Trans-nationalising Chineseness: Overseas Chinese Policies of the PRC's Central Government. Asien, 96, 7-28.

Bolt, P. (1996). Looking to the Diaspora: The Overseas Chinese and China's Economic Development, 1978-1994. Diaspora: A Journal of Transnational Studies, 5(3), 467-496.

Chin, K. & Smith, D. (2012). Immigrants, Diaspora and State Transnationalism: A Reconceptualization Illustrated via the South Korea-United States Connection. Global Networks, 15(1), 29 – 41.

China Daily (2008, March 30). Dalai clique's masterminding of Lhasa violence exposed. Retrieved from http://www.chinadaily.com.cn/china/2008-03/30/content_6576350.htm

China Daily (2018, January 23). New rules for visas to help Chinese 'return home'. Retrieved from chinadaily.com.cn/a/201801/23/WS5a668664a3106e7dcc135dfb.html

China Internet Information Center (2017). Press conference: CPC's united front and international relations. Retrieved from http://china.org.cn/china/2017-10/23/content_41777176.htm

Delano, A. & Mylonas, H. (2019): The microfoundations of diaspora politics: unpacking the state and disaggregating the diaspora. Journal of Ethnic and Migration Studies, 45(4), 473–491.

Die Presse (2008, March 15): Lhasa brennt – offene Revolte der Tibeter. Retrieved from https://diepresse.com/home/ausland/aussenpolitik/369970/Tibet_Lhasa-brennt-offene-Revolte-der-Tibeter

Europe Weekly (2009, September 9). Liuzhu yanhuang zisun de 'gen', 7.

Europe Weekly (2011a, January 24). Shandong shengwei shuji Jian Yikang shuai tuan fangao, 3.

Europe Weekly (2011b, February 7). Hongmei ying xuefang, yutu ta chunlai, 4.

Europe Weekly (2011c, September 19). Di liu jie shijie huawen meiti luntan zai Chongqing kaimu, 5.

Europe Weekly (2014a, January 3). Wei renmin fu, 1.

Europe Weekly (2014b, April 11). Lao qiaotuan yao huanyou qingchun, 4.

Europe Weekly (2014c, August 29). Aohua zonghui zhaokai quanti lishihui, 10.

Fransen, S. & Siegel, M. (2011). The Development of Diaspora Engagement Policies in Burundi and Rwanda. UNU-MERIT Working Papers, 2011-038.

Gamlen, A. (2008). The emigration state and the modern geopolitical imagination. Political Geography, 27, 840-856.

Gazsó, D. (2017). Diaspora Policies in Theory and Practice. Hungarian Journal of Minority Studies, 1, 65-87.

Gu, Y. (2017): Huaqiaohuaren lanpishu. Huaqiao huaren yanjiu baogao 2017. Beijing: Shehui kexue wenjian chubanshe.

Hamilton, C. (2018). Silent Invasion. China's influence in Australia. Victoria: Hardie Grant Books.

Henan Provincial Federation of Returned Overseas Chinese (2018, April 28). Aodili huaren zonghui fangwentuan lai He kaocha. Retrieved from www.henanql.org/NewsDetails.aspx?Id=4862

Hirn, W. (2012). Überseechinesen – Die fünfte Kolonne Pekings. Manager Magazin, 3. April 2012. Retrieved from http://www.manager-magazin.de/magazin/artikel/a-825249.html

Ho, E. (2011). 'Claiming' the diaspora: Elite mobility, sending state strategies and the spatialities of citizenship. Progress in Human Geography, 2011, 1–16.

Hughes, C. (2000). Nationalism in Chinese cyberspace. Cambridge Review of International Affairs, 13(2), 195-209.

Jacques, M. (2012). When China rules the world. New York: Pinguin Books.

Lin X. (2000): Shilun Huaqiao Huaren he Ao Xiang tongbao dui zuguo dalu de touzi ji qi falu baohu. Huaqiao Huaren Lishi Yanjiu, 2, 8.

Liu, H. & van Dongen, E. (2016). China's diaspora policies as a new mode of transnational governance. Journal of Contemporary China, 25(102), 805-821.

Nyiri, P. (1999). Chinese Organisations in Hungary, 1989-1996: A case study in PRC-oriented community politics overseas. In Pieke, F. & Mallee, H. (Eds.), Internal and International Migration: Chinese Perspectives. Richmond: Routledge, 251-279.

Nyiri, P. (2001). Expatriating is Patriotic? The Discourse on 'New Migrants' in the People's Republic of China. In Starrs, R. (Ed.), Asian Nationalism in an Age of Globalization (144-157). London: Routlegde, 635-653.

Nyiri, P. (2007). Chinese in Eastern Europe and Russia. A middleman minority in a transnational era. New York: Routledge.

Outuo (2008a, March 16). Wo suo zhidao de Lasa baoluan. Retrieved from www.outuo.net/vbulletin/showthread.php/22573-我所知道的拉萨暴乱-zt

Outuo (2008b, March 22). Huodong yi quxiao Retrieved from www.outuo.net/vbulletin/showthread.php/22909-活动已取消

Outuo (2008c, March 21). Zang du you yao qu shiguan youxing le. Retrieved from www.outuo.net/vbulletin/showthread.php/23462-藏独又要去使馆游行了－－KURIER报上发藏独的公告?p=260937&viewfull=1#post260937

Outuo (2008d, March 21). Lüdang juran huotong Zang du chongji wo shiguan!! Retrieved from www.outuo.net/vbulletin/showthread.php/22873-绿党居然伙同藏独冲击我使馆！！

Outuo (2008e, March 23). Jintian an fangle Zang du Weiyena judian – zhaopian. Retrieved from www.outuo.net/vbulletin/showthread.php/22940-今天暗访了藏独维也纳聚点-照片

Outuo (2008f, March 30). Munihei – wusheng de kangyi – wei zhi gandong. Retrieved from www.outuo.net/vbulletin/showthread.php/23427-慕尼黑-无声的抗议-为之感动

Outuó (2008g, March 31): 3 yue 31 ri Zang du zai Weiyena shiwei youxing de quancheng baodao. Retrieved from http://www.outuo.net/vbulletin/archive/index.php/t-23517.html

Outuo (2008h, April 17). Youxing zhaoji tie, zhengshi tongzhi. Retrieved from www.outuo.net/vbulletin/showthread.php/24426-游行召集贴，正式通知

Outuo (2008i, April 19). ORF dui youxing de xiangguan baogao. Retrieved from www.outuo.net/vbulletin/showthread.php/24613-ORF对游行的相关报道，以及脑残网友之评论！

Outuo (2010, October 26). Aodili jixu shangyan hairentingyan shijian, dangjie liuxue. Retrieved at www.outuo.net/vbulletin/showthread.php/62185-奥地利继续上演骇人听闻事件,当街血流-主角是本人(申请挂版头条数日）

Outuo (2014, March 18). Ouzhou huaren huaqiao tuixiuzhe xiehui. Retrieved from www.outuo.net/vbulletin/showthread.php/103773-欧洲华人华侨退休者协会-关于解决海外华人华侨国内退休金问题的呼吁-zt [13.10.2015].

People's Daily (2008, March 22). Crush "Tibet independence" forces' conspiracy, People's Daily urges. Retrieved from http://en.people.cn/90001/90776/6378810.html

Qiaoban (2006). Qiaowu gongzuo gailun. Beijing: Zhigongchubanshe.

Qingtian Wang (2018, January 31). Aodili huaren huaqiao lianyihui juxing zhonggong shijiu da jingshen xuexi xuanjiang hui ji. Retrieved from www.zgqt.zj.cn/news/text.asp?id=669997

Qiu, J. (2011): Huaqiaohuaren lanpishu. Huaqiao huaren yanjiu baogao 2011. Beijing: Shehui kexue wenjian chubanshe.

Qiu, J. (2012): Huaqiaohuaren lanpishu. Huaqiao huaren yanjiu baogao 2012. Beijing: Shehui kexue wenjian chubanshe.

Ragazzi, F. (2014). A comparative analysis of diaspora policies. Political Geography, 41, 74-89.

Renmin Ribao (2008, February 6). Aodili huaqiaohuaren xiying xinchun. Retrieved from http://world.people.com.cn/GB/6869509.html

Renmin Ribao (2018, August 24). Xiang shijie zhanguan zhenshi liti quanmian de Zhongguo. Retrieved from politics.people.com.cn/n1/2018/0824/c1001-30247603.html

Schäfer, C. (2018). "Nachfahren des Drachen" und "echte Wiener"? Identitäten und Inkorporationsmuster chinesischer Migranten in Österreich am Beispiel des Webforums www.outuo.net [Dissertation, University of Vienna]. Cologne China Studies Online (1).

Schunck, R. (2014). Transnational Activities and Immigrant Integration in Germany. Concurrent or Competitive Processes? Heidelberg: Springer.

Shen, I. (2006). A Century of Chinese Exclusion Abroad. Beijing: Foreign Language Press.

Sun, H., Zhang, Y. & Li, S. (2014). The 14th Dalai Lama. Peking: Foreign Language Press.

Thuno, M. (2001). Reaching Out and Incorporating Chinese Overseas: The Trans-territorial Scope of the PRC by the End of the 20th Century. China Quarterly, 168, 910-929.

Thinley, P. (2008). China salaries overseas Chinese for anti-Tibetan protests. April 19, 2008. Retrieved from www.phayul.com/news/article.aspx?id=20795

To, J. (2012). Beijing's Policies for Managing Han and Ethnic-Minority Chinese Communities Abroad. Journal of Current Chinese Affairs, 41, 183-221.

To, J. (2014). Qiaowu: Extra-Territorial Policies for the Overseas Chinese. Leiden: Brill.

Wang, H. (2017). Zhongguo quyu guoji rencai jingzhengli baogao. Beijing: Shehui kexue wenjian chubanshe.

West, C. (2014). Zwischen kulturellem Pluralismus und Transkulturalität –Postmoderne Momente im Migrationsdiskurs. Forschungsberichte der ARL 3. Retrieved from https://www.econstor.eu/bitstream/10419/141931/1/fb_003_07.pdf

Western Returned Scholars Association (2018, February 2018): Aodili huaqiaohuaren liu-xuesheng juxing 2018 nian xinchun wanhui. Retrieved from www.wrsa.net/content_40229993.htm

Xi, J. (2017). Xi Jinping qiaowu sixiang tanxi. Retrieved from www.wxyjs.org.cn/xxgcxjpzsjxljhjszl/gyfzshzymzzz/201707/t20170728_225025.html

Xinhua (2013, October 21). Xi Jinping: shi liuxuesheng renyuan huiguo you yongwuzhidi – liu zai haiwai you baoguo zhi men. Retrieved from www.xinhuanet.com/politics/2013-10/21/c_117808372.html

Yang A. (2010). From "Silent Memory" to Colective Protests in Real Life: Tension, Resistance and Online Identity Discourse of Overseas Chinese. Journal of Intercultural Communication, 1(22), no pagination.

Zhongguo Qiaowang (2014, June 6). Xi Jinping huijian di qi jie shijie huaqiaohuaren shetuan lianyi dahui dabiao. Retrieved from http://www.chinaqw.com/sqjg/2014/06-06/5705.shtml

CHAPTER 6
"OUT OF SIGHT, OUT OF MIND". MANAGING MIGRATION FLOWS WITH TURKEY AS A "SAFE THIRD COUNTRY"?

Annalisa Geraci

Introduction

Since 2015 an uncontrolled increase in the arrivals of migrants has not been followed by a shared response based on solidarity (Carrera *et al.*, 2015; Thielemann *et al.*, 2010). The so-called "refugee crisis" has highlighted the European Union's inability to address the issue of migration. Indeed, the initial empathy expressed by the Heads of State and Government of the Member States with regard to the serious shipwreck off the Libyan coast in April 2015 has given way to "externalization of migration and border controls" (Moreno-Lax & Giuffré, 2017:3).

The principle of solidarity and fair sharing of responsibility has been invoked by the Union as a whole, but some Member States have strongly opposed the decisions to redistribute migrant quotas (European Commission, 2017)[1.] These latter ones – ruled by populist and nationalist parties – are consciously exploiting the migration issue to propagate the European Union's inability to face migration crisis. On the basis of that inadequacy and the fluctuating results in burden-sharing activities (e.g. relocation and resettlement mechanisms)[2], the action – "Working in partnership with third countries to tackle migration upstream" outlined by the European Commission in the

---

1 The European Commission has referred Czech Republic, Hungary and Poland to the Court of Justice of the European Union (CJEU) for their refusal to accept refugee quotas under temporary emergency relocation scheme. The press release is available at http://europa.eu/rapid/press-release_IP-17-5002_en.htm.
2 Council Decision (EU) 2015/1523 of 14 September 2015 establishing provisional measures in the area of international protection for the benefit of Italy and of Greece; Council Decision (EU) 2015/1601 of 22 September 2015 establishing provisional measures in the area of international protection for the benefit of Italy and Greece.

European Agenda on migration – has gradually acquired a central role in managing the migration crisis (European Commission, 2015a). If on the one hand, there has been a lack of unity in the redistribution of burdens between Member States, on the other hand, these have shown a strong cooperation to encourage the partnership with third countries, such as Turkey, to manage migration flows outside the EU territory.

On 18 March 2016, with the EU-Turkey Statement, the European Council and Turkey established an understanding of nine action points to reduce irregular migration via the eastern Mediterranean route. This typical external tool, useful for overcoming the impasse in the Union's internal immobility, has drawn a great deal of criticism.

The analysis starting from the most controversial issues deals with the content of the statement (e.g. the return of all irregular migrants and the so-called "one-for-one scheme") and the relevant assumption that holds up and justifies a part of the EU-Turkey statement. Namely, the possible recognition of Turkey as a "safe third country" and a "first country of asylum". Subsequently, the focus will be on the safe country concepts and the possible modification of "safe third country" notion by analyzing the new proposal for a Regulation repealing the "Asylum Procedures Directive" (European Commission, 2016a).

The fundamental questions on this article are: can Turkey currently be qualified as a safe third country? Does Turkey meet the criteria set out in Article 38 (Asylum Procedures Directive)? Could the proposal for a Regulation repealing the "Asylum Procedures Directive" and the related alteration of the "safe third country" concept reduce the standards of protection for asylum seekers?

This article will demonstrate that Turkey, although it has changed its legal framework in the field of asylum, does not implement adequately its legislation. As we will see later, there are several analysis and reports that highlight numerous malfunctions of this conuntry´s asylum system (cases of arbitrary detention, risk of deportation to their country of origin, violations of the principle of non-refoulement, etc.). Finally, the article will highlight the choice made by the Union: to widen the security dimension (more shared by the Member States) rather than the humanitarian dimension.

The EU-Turkey Statement: Its Main Elements and Critical Issues

On 18 March 2016, in order "to end the irregular migration from Turkey to the EU" the European Council and Turkey reached a statement. Below the main operating procedures:

1. "all new irregular migrants crossing from Turkey into Greek islands as from 20 March 2016 will be returned to Turkey", including asylum-seekers with inadmissible applications. This is possible if Turkey is qualified as a "safe third country" or a "first country of asylum" by the Greek authorities. Therefore, this statement could allow not only to deport irregular migrants not in need of

international protection, but also Syrian refugees.

2. "for every Syrian being returned to Turkey from the Greek islands, another Syrian will be resettled to the EU", the so-called "one-for-one scheme" (European Council, 2016).

Observing these formulations, a twofold objective would seem to emerge: on the one hand, to deter any "irregular entry" [3] by returning migrants from Greece to Turkey and, on the other hand, to "reward" Syrian migrants that did not attempt irregular entry into Greek territory, by a resettlement mechanism (Favilli, 2016:6; Marotti & Marchegiani, 2016; Rizzo, 2017).

The so-called "1:1 scheme" has raised a number of concerns. First, about the specific reference to Syrian migrants, only they can be resettled in Europe. Therefore, this mechanism would favor a specific nationality: the Syrian one. In contravention of the prohibition of non-discrimination contained in Article 3 of the Geneva Convention, which requires "Contracting States" to "apply the provisions of [the] Convention to refugees without discrimination as [...] country of origin" (Rossi & Iafrate, 2016:216). Second, it is observed a different treatment given to migrants, as they are divided into those who did not attempt to reach Greece and those who arrived irregularly on the Greek coast. This distinction has determined a "conditional" right of asylum on the basis of migrants 'behavior. In this way, the "good" Syrian migrant is resettled while the "bad" Syrian migrant is returned to Turkey. But the right to international protection cannot be subordinated by the migrants' forms of entry into a Member State (Roman, 2016).

As regards the return of all irregular migrants to Turkish territory, several scholars, NGOs, and humanitarian organizations highlighted the problem of collective expulsions and the violation of the principle of *non-refoulement* . For these actors, these concerns are some of the effects of the EU-Turkey statement, which is formally aimed at breaking the business model of smugglers (European Council, 2016), but which is substantially aimed at containing the arrival of migrants and shifting EU responsibility. Nevertheless, EU Commission did not share the same view. The institution considered these returns in "accordance with the requirements stemming from EU and international law, and in full respect of the principle of non-refoulement" (European Commission, 2016b). The fundamental assumption the whole agreement is based on is that Turkey can be recognized as a "safe third country" or a "first country of asylum". For the European Commission Turkey should be qualified as a safe country (European Commission, 2015b).

---

3 It is interesting to note that the term "irregular migration", under the EU-Turkey Statement, covers at the same time asylum-seekers and all migrants who cross irregularly the Greek borders, although asylum seekers have a right of entry limited to the possibility of submitting an asylum application.

The Safe Third Country Concept. The Current Criteria of Directive 2013/32/EU and The (Possible) Future Changes to The Concept Through The Analysis of The New Proposal for A Regulation Repealing The "Asylum Procedures Directive" (Com(2016) 467 Final)

Since the 1990s, the safe country concepts were present within the Union context (Council of the EU, 1992). Subsequently, these notions were added to the Asylum Procedures Directive (2005) and, finally, in the recast of the Procedures Directive in 2013 (Roman et al., 2016). The current Procedures Directive provides different concepts of safe country: "safe country of origin", "first country of asylum" and "safe third country". For the fundamental aim of the EU-Turkey Statement i.e. deporting all irregular migrants (including applicants for international protection), the focus will be on the notions of "first country of asylum" (article 35 of the Procedures Directive) and "safe third country" (article 38). These, although not directly mentioned in the EU-Turkey statement, are central to judging the admissibility or not of an asylum application and, consequently, to reducing the burden on Member States to the detriment of third countries (Lehner, 2018: 5; Thielemann, 2018: 73). Before starting the analysis of these two concepts, it is useful to underline the possibility for the Member States – under article 33(2) of the Procedures Directive – to declare inadmissible an application for international protection based on the above concepts (Peers & Roman, 2016; Favilli, 2016). The "first country of asylum" notion makes clear that a third country can be qualified as such in two cases:

a) if the applicant "has been *recognised* in that country *as a refugee* and he or she can still avail himself/herself of that protection (emphasis added)" or,

b) if the applicant, alternatively, "enjoys sufficient protection in that country, including benefiting from the principle of *non-refoulement*".[4]

Moreover, under article 35 of the Procedures Directive, Member States may take account of the criteria of article 38(1) in applying the "first country of asylum" concept. Regarding the first criterion (a), Turkey cannot be qualified as a "first country of asylum"[5] because it does not provide, under the 1951 Geneva Convention, refugee status to Non-European seekers (Lehner, 2018: 5; Peers & Roman, 2016: 6), whereas the second option (b) could be applied. Turkey, formally, provides different forms of protection for non-European asylum seekers: the "conditional refugee status" or a "subsidiary protection". Instead, for Syrian asylum seekers the country recognizes a temporary protection status.

That said, there was no lack of criticism over the implementation and

---

4 Under article 35 of the Procedures Directive.
5 Under article 61 of the Turkish Law on Foreigners and International Protection (Law No. 6458 of 2013), Turkey provides the refugee status «only to refugees coming from Europe to Turkey as a consequence of Turkey's geographical limitation on the refugee definition provided under article 1A(2) of the Geneva Convention».

recognition of the forms of protection above mentioned[6] (Ilcan et al., 2018:59; Lehner, 2018:6; Favilli, 2016:10), as well as over the respect of principle of *non-refoulement* (Peers & Roman, 2016:7; AIDA, 2017). Whether or not to recognize Turkey as a "first country of asylum" is controversial.

Now with reference to the "safe country concept", what are the requirements that allow Member States to define whether a third country is "safe"? The Asylum Procedures Directive sets out different criteria under Article 38(1): "a) life and liberty [should] not [be] threatened on account of race, religion, nationality, membership of a particular social group or political opinion; (b) there [should be] no risk of serious harm as defined in Directive 2011/95/EU; (c) the principle of *non-refoulement* in accordance with the Geneva Convention [should be] respected; (d) the prohibition of removal, in violation of the right to freedom from torture and cruel, inhuman or degrading treatment as laid down in international law, [should be] respected; and e) [should] exist the possibility to request refugee status and, if found to be a refugee, to receive protection in accordance with the Geneva Convention".

Regarding the opportunity to recognize Turkey as a "safe third country", some scholars argued that Turkey does not allow the access to refugee protection to non-Europeans seekers and, among them, even Syrians, as enshrined in the Geneva Convention (Peers & Roman, 2016; Roman et al, 2016; Cherubini, 2017; Favilli, 2016). For Peers and Roman, it is arguable that the "safe third country" concept can only be interpreted as applying to countries that have ratified and fully applied the Geneva Convention. Moreover, Turkey seems not to fulfill other criteria (b, c, d) under article 38(1) because, as several reports have shown, in that country there have been deportations, push-backs, arbitrary detentions and physical violence against asylum-seekers (Amnesty International, 2015; Human Rights Watch, 2018). Other scholars had "counter-arguments" (Thym, 2016) and/or more flexible positions about the chance to qualify Turkey as safe (among others: Lehner, 2018; Leghtas, 2017; Ulusoy & Battjes, 2017; Dimitriadi, 2016). Indeed, these latter ones focused more on the protection "in practice" than the legal qualification of the forms of protection. Hence, the questions are, in particular, related to the problems raised in the implementation phase of the Turkish asylum system; the respect of the principle of *non-refoulement* for Syrians; the possibility to "equalize" temporary protection to the standards of the Geneva Convention, regarding access to education, labor market and social assistance. It is not simple to examine the application of the law, but it is necessary to fully understand the usefulness and validity of the tool, i.e. the "EU-Turkey Statement".

In order to focus on the concepts of "first country of asylum" and "safe third country", we will now examine the Commission's proposal for an Asylum Procedures Regulation (European Commission, 2016a). The prospective

---

6 As regards the implementation and recognition of the forms of protection of asylum seekers in Turkey, see following sessions of the present work.

change of the Asylum Procedures Directive into a Regulation could represent a paradigm shift in the field of the Common European Asylum System (ASGI, 2017). The fundamental aim should be the harmonization of the current different procedural arrangements of the Member States through a common procedure. However, in this context, we raise a question: are we moving towards an improvement or a weakening of current protection standards? It is probably the second one, in particular about the criteria to qualify a third country as safe. As regards this notion, the EU Commission has proposed amendments of the present article 38(1) APD. In fact, the "new" article 45 could *oblige* Member States to apply the safe third country concept establishing a different criterion from that set out in Article 38(1)(e). Indeed, the revised proposal could determine a reduction in terms of standards of protection currently provided by the Procedures Directive, thanks to this new criterion (e): "the possibility to receive protection in accordance with *the substantive standards* of the Geneva Convention *or sufficient protection* as referred to in Article 44(2), as appropriate" (emphasis added).

On the new wording proposed by the EU Commission, the LIBE Committee (2018) approved several amendments. First, as regards the obligation to designate a third country as safe: the Committee proposed a change to remove this duty. Second, the same body also deleted the EU Commission's criterion (e) and, in the same time, added new subparagraphs from (ea) to (eg), (LIBE Committee, 2018). Some of the most important amendments adopted by the Committee at first reading are: "(ed) effective protection remains available until a durable solution can be found; (ef) the third country has acceded to international refugee instruments and basic human rights instruments and complies with their standards in practice; (eg) it is possible to request refugee status and, if found to be a refugee, to *receive protection in accordance with the Geneva Convention, ratified and applied without any geographical limitations,* or to request and *receive effective protection* within the meaning of points (a) to (g)" (emphasis added). The LIBE Committee's position is clear: it is fundamental for Member States to check whether the third country meets the criteria of the safe third country concept not just in form but also in substance. In other words, if the third state complies (or not) "in practice" with the essential human rights tools and international refugee instruments. Another interesting aspect is the possibility to obtain protection under the terms of the Geneva Convention, ratified and applied without any geographical limitation (article 45(1)(eg)). Maybe, these latter amendments have taken on board the criticisms made by some scholars and NGOs regarding the present application of the safe third country concept.

Conversely, the Commission's proposal seems to move towards lowering the guarantees of protection for refugees (Chetail, 2016). Obviously, through this new proposal the EU Commission is going to save the EU-Turkey Statement as well as the current and future EU external action with third countries by changing the criteria of the "safe third country" concept. Said that, it is not surprising that, for the EU Commission, this notion could also be applied to vulnerable subjects (such as unaccompanied minors). On this issue, the LIBE Committee amended the draft article 45(5) as follows: "The concept of safe third country *shall not be applied* to unaccompanied minors *unless it is determined to be clearly in their best interests*" (emphasis added). Moreover, with reference to the specific inclusion of Turkey in the list of safe countries of origin (annex 1 of the EU Commission proposal), the LIBE Committee's position did not leave the door open to different interpretations: Turkey should not be included in that list (LIBE Committee, 2018). Clearly, these two positions are not the same. On the one hand, there is the LIBE Committee that would strengthen the standards of refugee protection and, on the other hand, there is the EU Commission that seems to diminish the protection for asylum seekers. In other words, the question is whether the current article 38(1)(e), and its guarantees, could be replaced by draft article 45(1)(e) and its ambiguous and less demanding formula: "substantive standards of the Geneva Convention or sufficient protection" (Chetail, 2016).

It will then be necessary to verify what will happen in the subsequent stages of discussion of the proposal. At first stage, a compromise position by presidency of the Council of the European Union would seem to emerge: establishing the lists of "first countries of asylum" and "safe third countries" at a European level and, at the same time, maintaining the lists at a national level. However, we wonder whether it would be useful to have national and European lists at the same time or whether this could create confusion, between the two levels and, above all, in the application of the two qualifications.

Turkish Legal Framework in The Field of Asylum

Turkey is having a key role in managing the current refugee crisis, but this country should not have been the only one. The European Union would have had to manage the flow of migrants; but since 2015 it has been showing that it is not able to handle the so-called "refugee crisis" internally. In other words, the EU has demonstrated all its powerlessness and the lack of political will to manage the large flows by sharing responsibility (Zaragoza-Cristiani, 2015). We wonder whether Turkey is a safe country for asylum seekers and, in particular, for Syrians. First, does it provide minimum standards of protection? Second, what kind of protection does it offer? Third, if it recognizes not only de jure, but also de facto, the rights associated with the different forms of protection. Before attempting to answer these questions, it is necessary to highlight that Turkey, for the fourth consecutive year, has hosted the largest number of refugees worldwide with 3.5 million people (UNHCR, 2018: 3), being most of them Syrians (3,424,200). Thus, it is important to consider not only the qualitative elements of the event but also the quantitative ones, especially because the quantitative elements allow us to capture the size of the phenomenon, such as the Turkish one.

Over the years the malfunctioning of the asylum system in Turkey has been widely discussed (among others: Farcy, 2015; Kirisci, 2007; Latif, 2002). However, Turkey has recently approved a new legislation on asylum, namely the "Law on Foreigners and International Protection Act" 2013 (LFIP). From the outset, this received the assent by UNHCR and some NGOs that confirmed the human rights-based approach (UNHCR, 2013). The LFIP establishes three types of protection: "refugee status", "conditional refugee status" and "subsidiary protection". The first form of protection recognizes the "refugee status", under the Geneva Convention, to asylum seekers from European countries (article 61, LFIP). Hence, this protection cannot be recognized to Syrian refugees. The second one, i.e. "conditional refugee status", is addressed to a person who arrived from non-European countries, contrary to "refugee status". Nevertheless, Syrians are excluded even from this kind of protections because they have a specific legal framework. For these subjects, in 2014, Turkey adopted the Temporary Protection Regulation (TPR) based on Article 91(LFIP). The differences between "conditional refugee protection" and "refugee protection" are highlighted by the lack of rights, related to a long-term integration and family reunification, for the first status.

The third form of protection, i.e. subsidiary, is addressed to individuals that cannot be recognized as "refugees" or as beneficiaries of a "conditional refugee status". "Subsidiary protection" shall be granted to persons who: a) would be sentenced to death or face the execution of the death penalty; b) would face torture or inhuman or degrading treatment or punishment; c) would face serious threat to himself or herself by reason of indiscriminate violence in situations of international or nationwide armed conflict, if they were returned to their country of origin (article 63, LFIP). This type of status is similar to "subsidiary protection" under Directive 2011/95/EU, as well. In Turkey, this protection does not cover all the rights granted by refugee status, indeed, with the first one, the person is excluded from long-term legal integration in Turkish territory as a "conditional refugee protection" (AIDA, 2017: 97).

As above mentioned, Turkey has recognized a specific protection for Syrians, the "temporary protection". This status is granted to "foreigners who have been forced to leave their country, cannot return to the country that they have left, and have arrived at or crossed the borders of Turkey in a mass influx situation seeking immediate and temporary protection" (under article 91 LFIP). The temporary regulation has defined the principles, the procedures, the rights and duties for Syrians, from the observance of non-refoulement principle (article 6, TPR) to the access to social services, such as healthcare, education, and labor market access. The TPR has represented a great step forward for the protection of Syrians. Nevertheless, there are still discrepancies in treatment between those who have "refugee status" and those who have "temporary protection", i.e. Syrians who returned under EU-Turkey Statement. Indeed, it is very clear, under article 7 TPR, that the "persons benefiting from temporary protection shall not be deemed as having been directly acquired one of the international protection statuses as defined in the Law" (emphasis added). What are the most obvious differences between "refugee status" and "temporary protection status"? One of the most important distinction is that with "temporary protection status" Syrians cannot benefit from "the right to long term residence permit" and they cannot "apply for Turkish citizenship" (under article 25 TPR). In this regard, some scholars have highlighted how often, with the aim of providing protection to asylum seekers, an "ambiguous architecture of precarity" has been created for them, about their status, their space and their freedom of movement (Ilcan et al., 2018). The temporary protection regime for Syrians and the related rights and restrictions inevitably contribute to an increased sense of precariousness.

It is to be welcomed that Turkey has endowed itself with a clear legal framework that have defined the types of protection for asylum seekers, even though Syrians are granted temporary protection and not refugee protection status. After analyzing the forms of protection provided by Turkish law, could we affirm that temporary protection is comparable to refugee status under the Geneva Convention (in terms of social assistance, access to education and access to the labor market)? In other words, beyond the geographical reservation, beyond the more or less restrictive interpretation of the concept of "safe third country" under Article 38 (EU Procedures Directive): could we affirm that Turkey offers, in practice, protection comparable to refugee status?

The next session will look at whether Turkey is correctly implementing the regulation on temporary protection, or whether there are implementation problems, especially with regard to respect for human rights.

Turkish Asylum System: A Focus on Temporary Protection Regime and Human Rights Violations

The TPR is a secondary legislation, based on article 91 LFIP which has established that the Council of Ministers shall define the actions for the reception of foreigners, their rights and obligations, their stay in Turkey and their exit from this country, etc. This is the first problem that emerges from the analysis of the temporary protection regime. The rights, obligations and measures established by the Council of Ministers should normally be laid down in a proper law. In fact, this creates a situation of great uncertainty and insecurity for the recipients of temporary protection (NOAS, 2016; AIDA, 2017). This regime could easily change legal attributes because of political changes, especially in a country where the state of emergency lasted from July 2016 to July 2018. In 2016 the Special Representative of the Secretary General on migration, Tomáš Boček, underlined a "lack of clarity" about the duration of the temporary protection regime. Furthermore, this precarious dimension could lead Syrians to try to arrive in Europe with the risk of being repatriated to Turkey (Baban et al., 2016). In short, its vagueness could lead to a vicious circle.

As regards the respect of the non-refoulement (article 6 TPR), several reports complain the substantial breach of that principle (Amnesty International, 2016; Human Rights Watch, 2018; Tomáš Boček, 2016; Council of Europe Parliamentary Assembly, 2016). This last Institution confirmed that "there have been reports of onward refoulement of both Syrians and non-Syrians" in Turkey, and for this the Institution recommended refraining from any further refoulement of asylum seekers returned from Greece. Yet, Human Rights Watch (2018) denounced summary rejections "to the war-ravaged Idlib governorate in Syria".

With regard to the public services that shall be provided to persons under temporary protection (such as health care, education, access to work, etc.), it can be argued that such rights are covered by TPR. Nevertheless, there are not certainties on how these social services shall be provided and administrated by government agencies. So far, its ambiguous dimension has led to differentiated treatments in access to these rights (Rygiel et al., 2016; Ineli-Ciger, 2015). Some problems with access to health care have occurred in some cities where Syrians have been asked to pay social safety premiums (TTB, 2014). Moreover, the "non-camp" Syrian refugees had many problems in accessing basic social services (Council of Europe Parliamentary Assembly, 2016: 8). Other difficulties arose with the registration procedure for the issue of identity cards to Syrians (kimlik in Turkish) needed to access rights related to temporary protection.

The right of education is enshrined in article 28 TPR that recognizes the access to elementary and higher education to temporary protection beneficiaries. However, in practice, several families have underlined many obstacles to enter their children into Turkish schools due to social and language barriers. This, especially in the case of families that live outside of the camps where only 14% of children are in school (Kutlu, 2015). Moreover, according to a study by Human Rights Watch (2017), discrepancies were identified between the funds dedicated to Syrians children education by donors and the concrete amounts reported in the budgets.

Another element that should not be overlooked in order to understand whether the current Turkish system of protection can be valid, or not, is certainly the right to work. Ilcan, Rygiel and Baban (2018:62) have affirmed that this right is "one of the most important sources of precarity for Syrian refugees". Formally, the right of access to labor market services is enshrined in article 29 of the TPR. Also, in this case the procedures and the principles regarding the employment of persons under temporary protection are determined by the Council of Ministers (Turkish Council of Ministers, 2016). Syrians, under temporary protection, can apply for a work permit 6 months after their registration and, thanks to this document, they have the right to work and to benefit from economic and social rights. However, the possibility for Syrians to be included in the economic and social fabric of Turkey runs counter to the concrete implementation of such inclusion. Since 2016, only about 7,700 work permits have been issued to Syrians. After the regulation on the work permits, the number of authorizations has increased to 13,298. Nevertheless, the number of irregular Syrian workers still remains very high, about 500,000 to 1,000,000 (Goksel, 2017; Kadkoy, 2017:2). The phenomenon of irregular workers is particularly insidious: not only for the State concerned, which is not able to have an idea of the magnitude of the phenomenon, but also for the subjects affected by this practice. Irregular workers typically face problems such as: exploitation, unsafe working conditions, lack of payment of wages, abuses, etc. (ILO, 2017).

We cannot say that Turkey has not made progress in establishing a comprehensive asylum system, especially for Syrians who cannot be protected under the Geneva Convention. However, as demonstrated above, the application of the "Law on Foreigners and International Protection Act" and the TPR remain problematic in practice. In general terms, there are still a number of critical issues within the Turkish asylum system such as violations of non-refoulement principle, arbitrary detention, infringements of procedural rights, etc. In some cases, temporary accommodation camps were de facto detention camps for Syrian refugees (Amnesty International, 2016b:110; Boček, 2016:28). The detentions have also been imposed to temporary protection recipients who violated their obligation to stay in their province (AIDA, 2017:120). Some NGOs and the civil society organizations have reported several difficulties in Turkey related to securing legal representation and cases of deprivation of the liberty for asylum seekers (Amnesty International, 2016b:16).

Recently, the European Parliament has expressed "its deep concern at the ongoing deterioration in fundamental rights and freedoms and the rule of law in Turkey" (European Parliament, 2018). Indeed, after the failed military coup in Turkey, a sense of uncertainty and insecurity has also gradually grown among Turkish citizens (Sirkeci, 2017:129).

Therefore, in spite of the question of whether or not Turkey is a safe third country, another question could be raised: how can Turkey be "safe" for asylum seekers and, at the same time, be an "insecure" country for its citizens? This country is facing a great challenge, managing migration flows. Some progress has been made, but the asylum system needs to be improved in its implementation; the international protection must be guaranteed.

The European Union, for its part, could have played a central role to manage the "refuge crisis", but, as it has shown in recent years, fully shared responses and actions have all been directed towards the outsourcing of the asylum policy.

References

Amnesty International. (2016b). International Community and Refugees: Responsibilities, Possibilities, Human Rights Violations. Istanbul: Amnesty International Turkey. Available at https://www.amnesty.org.tr/uploads/Docs/en_12_11_27122016_baski149.pdf

Amnesty International. (2016a). Turkey: Illegal mass returns of Syrian refugees expose fatal flaws in EU-Turkey deal. Available at https://www.amnesty.org/en/press-releases/2016/04/turkey-illegal-mass-returns-of-syrian-refugees-expose-fatal-flaws-in-eu-turkey-deal/.

Amnesty International. (2015). Europe's gatekeeper: Unlawful detention and deportation of

refugees from Turkey. Available at
https://www.amnesty.org/en/documents/eur44/3022/2015/en/.

ASGI. (2017). Verso il nuovo Regolamento Procedure. Quale idea di Europa? Focus n.1: Il
concetto di paese terzo sicuro. Available at https://www.asgi.it/regolamento-procedure-ue-
paese-sicuro/.

Asylum Information Database (AIDA), 'Country Report Turkey' (2017). Available at
https://www.asylumineurope.org/sites/default/files/report-
download/aida_tr_2017update.pdf.

Baban F., Ilcan S., and Rygiel K. (2016). Syrian refugees in Turkey: Pathways to precarity,
differential inclusion, and negotiated citizenship rights. Journal of Ethnic and Migration
Studies. DOI: 10.1080/1369183X.2016.1192996.

Boček, T. (2016). Report of the fact-finding mission to Turkey by Ambassador Tomáš Boček,
Special Representative of the Secretary General on migration and refugees, 30 May – 4 June
2016 [SG/Inf(2016)29]. Available at https://www.ecoi.net/en/document/1353541.html.

Carrera, S., Blockmans, S., Gros, D., & Guild, E. (2015). The EU's Response to the Refugee
Crisis: Taking Stock and Setting Policy Priorities. CEPS Essay, (20/16). Available at SSRN:
http://ssrn.com/abstract=2715460.

Cherubini, F. (2017). The "EU-Turkey Statement" of 18 March 2016: A (Umpteenth?)
Celebration of Migration Outsourcing. In: Baldin S., Zago M. (eds), Europe of Migrations:
Policies, Legal Issues and Experiences, Trieste: EUT Edizioni Università di Trieste, 32-47.

Chetail, V. (2016). Looking beyond the Rhetoric of the Refugee Crisis: The Failed Reform of
the Common European Asylum System. European Journal of Human Rights, 584-602.
Available at SSRN: https://ssrn.com/abstract=2898063.

Council of Europe Parliamentary Assembly. (2016). The situation of refugees and migrants
under the EU-Turkey Agreement of 18 March 2016, Resolution No. 2106.

Council of the EU. (1992). Resolution of 30 November 1992 on a Harmonized Approach to
Questions Concerning Host Third Countries ("London Resolution"). Available at
http://www.refworld.org/docid/3f86c3094.html.

Dimitriadi, A. (2016). The Impact of the EU-Turkey Statement on Protection and Reception:
The Case of Greece. Global Turkey in Europe Project, No. 15. Rome. Available at
http://www.iai.it/en/pubblicazioni/impact-eu-turkey-statement-protection-and-reception-
case-greece.

European Commission. (2017). Relocation: Commission refers the Czech Republic, Hungary
and Poland to the Court of Justice. Press release is available at
http://europa.eu/rapid/press-release_IP-17-5002_en.htm.

European Commission. (2016c). Communication on Establishing a New Partnership
Framework with Third Countries Under the European Agenda on Migration, COM (2016)
385 final.

European Commission. (2016b). First Report on the progress made in the implementation of
the EU-Turkey Statement. Brussels, 20.4.2016, COM(2016) 231 final.

European Commission. (2016a). Proposal for a regulation of the European Parliament and of
the Council establishing a common procedure for international protection in the Union and
repealing Directive 2013/32/EU. Brussels, 13.7.2016, COM(2016) 467 final.

European Commission. (2015b). Proposal for a regulation of the European Parliament and of
the Council establishing an EU common list of safe countries of origin for the purposes of
Directive 2013/32/EU of the European Parliament and of the Council on common
procedures for granting and withdrawing international protection, and amending Directive
2013/32/EU. Brussels, 9.9.2015 COM(2015) 452 final.

European Commission. (2015a). A European Agenda on Migration. Communication from the
Commission to the European Parliament, the Council, the European Economic and Social
Committee and the Committee of the Regions. Brussels, 13.5.2015, COM (2015) 240 final.

European Council. (2016). EU-Turkey statement, 18 March 2016, General Secretariat of the
Council, Press release, 144/16.

European Parliament. (2018). Current human rights situation in Turkey. European Parliament resolution of 8 February 2018 on the current human rights situation in Turkey. (2018/2527(RSP)). Available at http://www.europarl.europa.eu/sides/getDoc.do?pubRef=-//EP//TEXT+TA+P8-TA-2018-0040+0+DOC+XML+V0//EN.

Farcy, J. B. (2015). EU-Turkey agreement: solving the EU asylum crisis or creating a new Calais in Bodrum. EU Migration Law Blog, 7 December 2015.

Favilli, C. (2016). La cooperazione UE-Turchia per contenere il flusso dei migranti e richiedenti asilo: obiettivo riuscito. Diritti umani e diritto internazionale, 2.

Goksel, G. U. (2017). Integration of Immigrants and the Theory of Recognition: 'Just Integration'. Palgrave Macmillan. 145-175.

Human Rights Watch (2018). Turkey: Mass Deportations of Syrians EU Should Raise Issue, Pledge Aid at Conference. Available at https://www.hrw.org/news/2018/03/22/turkey-mass-deportations-syrians.

Human Rights Watch. (2017). Syrian Refugee Children's Uncertain School Aid. Murky Money Trail, Missed Targets, Missing Data. Available at https://www.hrw.org/news/2017/09/14/syrian-refugee-childrens-uncertain-school-aid.

Ilcan, S., Rygiel, K., & Baban, F. (2018). The ambiguous architecture of precarity: temporary protection, everyday living and migrant journeys of Syrian refugees. International Journal of Migration and Border Studies, 4(1-2), 51-70.

International Labor Organization - ILO. (2017). Informal economy. Available at http://www.ilo.org/global/topics/employment-promotion/informal-economy/lang-en/index.htm.

Ineli-Ciger, M. (2015). Implications of the new Turkish law on foreigners and international protection and regulation No. 29153 on temporary protection for Syrians seeking protection in Turkey, Oxford Monitor of Forced Migration, Vol. 4, No. 2, 28–36.

Kadkoy, O. (2017). Syrians and Labor Market Integration: Dynamics in Turkey and Germany. The German Marshall Fund of the United States. Available at http://www.gmfus.org/publications/syrians-and-labor-market-integration-dynamics-turkey-and-germany.

Kirişçi, K. (2007). The limits of conditionality and Europeanization: Turkey's dilemmas in adopting the EU acquis on asylum. Montreal, Canada. Available at http://aei.pitt.edu/7936/.

Kutlu, Z. (2015). From the Ante-Chamber to the Living Room: A Brief Assessment on NGO's Doing Work for Syrian Refugees. Istanbul: Anadolu Kultur and Acik Toplum Vakfi (Open Society Foundation). Available at http://www.anadolukultur.org.

Latif, D. (2002). Refugee policy of the Turkish Republic. The Turkish Year Book, 33, 12.

Leghtas, I. (2017). Like a Prison: Asylum Seekers Confined to the Greek Islands. Available at https://reliefweb.int/sites/reliefweb.int/files/resources/201708%2BGreece_PDF_DRAFT%2BTWO.pdf.

Lehner, R. (2018). The EU-Turkey-'deal': Legal Challenges and Pitfalls. Int. Migr. doi:10.1111/imig.12462.

LIBE Committee. (2018). Report on the proposal for a regulation of the European Parliament and of the Council establishing a common procedure for international protection in the Union and repealing Directive 2013/32/EU. A8-0171/2018.

Marotti, L., & Marchegiani, M. (2016). L'accordo tra l'Unione europea e la Turchia per la gestione dei flussi migratori: cronaca di una morte annunciata?. Diritto, immigrazione e cittadinanza, 1(1/2): 59-82.

Moreno-Lax, V., & Giuffré, M. (2017). The Rise of Consensual Containment: From 'Contactless Control' to 'Contactless Responsibility' for Forced Migration Flows, S. Juss (ed.), Research Handbook on International Refugee Law (Edward Elgar, Forthcoming). Available at SSRN: https://ssrn.com/abstract=3009331.

NOAS - Norwegian Organisation for Asylum Seekers. (2016). Seeking Asylum in Turkey: A Critical Review of Turkey's Asylum Laws and Practices, Available at http://www.noas.no/wp-content/uploads/2016/04/NOAS-rapport-Tyrkia-april-2016.pdf.

Peers, S., & Roman, E. (2016). The EU, Turkey and the Refugee Crisis: What could possibly go wrong?.EU Law Analysis, 5.

Rizzo, A. (2017). La dimensione esterna dello spazio di libertà, sicurezza e giustizia. Sviluppi recenti e sfide aperte. Freedom, Security & Justice: European Legal Studies, 1: 147-177.

Roman, E., Baird T.E., & Radcliffe, T. (2016). Why Turkey is Not a "Safe Country". Statewatch Analysis, No 3/16, February 2016, Available online at: statewatch.org.

Rossi, E., & Iafrate, P. (2016). Il sistema di asilo europeo ei diritti umani dei rifugiati: verso una regressione?. Revista Gênero & Direito, 5(2).

Rygiel, K., Baban, F., & Ilcan, S. (2016). The Syrian refugee crisis: The EU-Turkey 'deal' and temporary protection. Global Social Policy, 16(3), 315-320.

Sirkeci, I. (2017). Turkey's refugees, Syrians and refugees from Turkey: a country of insecurity. Migration Letters, 14(1), 127-144.

Spijkerboer, T. (2017). Bifurcation of people, bifurcation of law: externalization of migration policy before the EU Court of Justice. Journal of Refugee Studies, 31(2), 216-239.

Thielemann, E. (2018). Why Refugee Burden-Sharing Initiatives Fail: Public Goods, Free-Riding and Symbolic Solidarity in the EU. JCMS: Journal of Common Market Studies, 56: 63–82. doi: 10.1111/jcms.12662.

Thielemann, E. R., Williams, R. and Boswell, C. (2010). What system of burden-sharing between Member States for the reception of asylum seekers? PE 419.620. European Parliament, Brussels, Belgium.

Thym, D. (2016). Why the EU-Turkey Deal is Legal and a Step in the Right Direction. Verfassungsblog. Available at https://verfassungsblog.de/why-the-eu-turkey-deal-is-legal-and-a-step-in-the-right-direction/.

TTB - Turkish Association of Medical Practitioners. (2014). Suriyeli Siginmacilar ve Saglik Raporu, Turk Tabipleri Birligi, Ankara.

Turkish Council of Ministers. (2016). Regulation regarding the Work Permits of Foreigners Provided with Temporary Protection. Available at: http://www.refworld.org/docid/582c71464.html.

Ulusoy, O., & Battjes, H. (2017). Situation of Readmitted Migrants and Refugees from Greece to Turkey under the EU-Turkey Statement. VU Migration Law Series No, 15, 1-42.

UNHCR. (2018). Global Trends: Forced Displacement in 2017. Available at http://www.unhcr.org/5b27be547.

UNHCR. (2013). UNHCR Welcomes Turkey's New Law on Asylum. Available at http://www.unhcr.org/news/briefing/2013/4/5167e7d09.

Vitiello, D. (2016). La dimensione esterna della politica europea. In: Savino, M. (ed.), La crisi migratoria tra Italia e Unione europea. Napoli, 333-354.

Zaragoza-Cristiani, J. (2015). Analysing the Causes of the Refugee Crisis and the Key Role of Turkey: Why Now and Why So Many? Working paper, RSC, RSCAS 2015/95, Robert Schuman Centre for Advanced Studies, BORDERLANDS Project.

CHAPTER 7
SOFT LAW, EFFECTIVENESS OF FUNDAMENTAL RIGHTS AND MIGRATION: HOW EFFECTIVE ARE MIGRANTS' FUNDAMENTAL RIGHTS IN AN ERA OF EUROPEAN GOVERNANCE?

Roila Mavrouli

Introduction

The objective of this research paper is to examine the valorization of procedural rationality in the field of fundamental rights related to migration from non-EU countries. This is in the context of an EU which is strengthening its constitutional nature, which sees a transition from the concept of government to the concept of governance. In this legal environment it is crucial to guarantee the effectiveness of fundamental rights, thus increasing their normative scope with regard to migration. The challenge to European governance practices and structures is how to transform the valorization of procedural rationality to essential rationality. This leads the democratic praxis to re-appropriate its origin. Nevertheless, this concept of procedural rationality establishes soft law as the fastest and most flexible solution to the migration challenge. The instruments of protection of fundamental rights have led to the systematic circumvention or deviation of rights[1]. In particular, this has been through the systematization of procedures related to detention and return. This has given rise to questions around an apparent conflict between democracy and bureaucracy, to the apparent detriment of democratic norms. In other words,

---

[1] The french "contournement de droits" refers to a repetitive practice of circumvention or deviation of rights in order to establish that practice as the normality. See Basilien-Gainche M.-L. (2015). The concept of exception state is indicative as it illustrates the paradigm of "every rule has an exception". In case of aggravating circumstances of crisis, the institutions are not capable of functionning normally and they need to suspend provisionnaly the existing law in force. This provisional suspension of law in force is considered to be acceptable in order to restore the legal order. See on this topic Basilien-Gainche M.-L. (2013).

if soft law seems to be the solution for migration, how can we assure the effectiveness of fundamental rights?

If the concept of sovereignty seems to be set aside in order to consolidate the transition of national government to European governance, national courts and especially the Karlsruhe Court can be reluctant to conform. Karlsruhe Court's decision of 30 June 2009 specifies that democratic legitimation exists only at a national level. In order to discuss this approach, our analysis will explore the democratic legitimation of European governance in the specific field of migration, viewed through the problematics of how the softening of a legal order might be a sign of the weakness of its normative power.

Even if most of CJEU decisions foster a constitutionalizing interpretation of EU powers, our analysis tends to question the effectiveness of fundamental rights in terms of migration, which are characterized by the intense use of soft law. If this illuminates the transition from forms of traditional government to a form of European governance (Peters, 2011), a relative effectiveness of fundamental rights within national contexts can confirm the emergence of a relativism of values. The inter-subjectivity of rights, which until now was essential, becomes communicational in order to achieve a high level of democratic procedural rationality (Habermas, 2004).

This paper argues how and why the question of migration highlights notions such as internal borders and a person's identification with a specific territory, ideas which are closely related to State sovereignty. This is despite Member States and the EU collaborating to maximise control of migratory flows. At a first level, the paper asserts the elements demonstrating the evolution of migration flow control into migration flow management. This results from a transition from the traditional model of government to the model of European governance. At a second level, the paper stresses the question of soft law as part of the model of European governance and if it strengthens or not the effectiveness of fundamental rights. The hypothesis is that soft law weakens the normativity of a legal order, ergo the effectiveness of fundamental rights. This reduces fundamental rights to a matter of a rational procedure and not to an essential element. In so doing it gives these policies the appearance of being perceived by citizens as being "normal". The hypothesis will be based on four elements: (i) a systematization of detention practices within national contexts, (ii) an increased number of soft law agreements between Member States and third-countries, (iii) the ambiguity of the terms "camp" or "hotspot" as a result of the denationalization process and, (iv) the externalization of European borders which results in avoiding the application of fundamental rights or not.

Systematization of Detention Practices

The question of migration interrogates the pre-established area of free movement of goods and people, and brings into question traditional concepts of State and Sovereignty. At the same time the EU expects a migration law to be applied based on EU agreements, pointing towards transition from the traditional form of national or intergovernmental governance to a new form of

EU governance. The blockage of national sovereignties by the concept of European governance results in a disruption of the concept of sovereignty when related to migration. This is because migration goes to the central core of sovereignty, national identity and attachment to a specific territory. At the same time, Member States are returning to take sovereign decisions when they have to deal with migration. The example of penalization of illegal entry within the French legal framework affirms national sovereignty and identification with a specific territory and challenges the pluralism of peoples of Europe, a pluralism that challenges and weakens national borders[2]. In this sense, migration crisis could be the inverse of a European governance crisis. In addition, the extensive use of soft law within the European context[3], as this paper will argue, cannot counterbalance strong sovereign decisions such as the reintroduction of border police in the Schengen area and the systematization of detention practices.

If we take the example of French Law, there are several enumerated categories of migrants that are eligible to a legal stay[4]. If the migrants do not fit to one of those categories as specified in the Ceseda Code, they are considered to have entered illegally (L.621-2(1)). Illegal residence has been abrogated in France, but illegal entry and facilitation of illegal residence[5] still exist as offenses.

---

2 Until now sovereignty and borders were associated to the traditional Nation-State and to a demos understood in a striclty ethno-cultural sense. The European polity came to change that through the effort to construct a European demos, namely a society of peoples of Europe as subjects of rights and representation. However, with regard to the EU demos, European citizens seem to distrust the EU institutions according to the "White Paper on European Governance" published by the Commission in 2001. In this sense, on the one hand, national identity and borders are still correlated with the traditional form of sovereingty but on the other hand, being part of the European project creates a pluralism that contradicts the initial traditional forms of sovereignty and people. On the subject of Europe and the people see Joly M. (2007).

3 Soft law instruments with regard to migration such as the regional agreements, the bilateral agreements, the IMO recommendations, the New York Declaration, the EU-Turkey Statement.

4 The French Ceseda Code classifies several categories that can be attributed a residence permit (provisional or permanent. For example according to the Ceseda Code, eligible to a legal entry, and ergo, eligible to a residence permit are those third-country nationals who are parents of a French child (article L.313-11-6° Ceseda), those third-country nationals who are husband/wife of a French citizen (article L.313-11-4° Ceseda), those third country-nationals who contribute to the intellectual, scientific, cultural and sports development of France (article L.315-1 Ceseda).

5 The concept of illegal entry is specified in article L-621-2(1) of the French Ceseda (Code of Entry and Residence of Aliens and the Right of Asylum) :"A foreign national who is not a national of a Member State of the European Union shall be liable to a sentence of one year's imprisonment and a fine of EUR 3 750: 1. if he has entered the territory of Metropolitan France without satisfying the conditions referred to in Article 5(1)(a), (b) and (c) of [the Schengen Borders Code] and without having been admitted to that territory pursuant to Article 5(4)(a) and (c) of that [code]; the same shall apply where an alert has been issued for the purpose of refusing the foreign national entry pursuant to an enforceable decision adopted by another State party to the [CISA]; 2. or if, arriving directly from the territory of a State party to [the CISA], he has entered the territory of Metropolitan France without complying with the requirements of Article 19(1) or (2), Article 20(1) and Article 21(1) or (2) thereof, with the exception of the conditions referred to in Article 5(1)(e) of [the Schengen Borders Code] and in Article 5(1)(d) where the alert for the purpose of refusing entry does not result from an enforceable decision adopted by another State party to the [CISA];". If the migrants do not fit to one of these categories as specified in the Ceseda (Code of Entry and Residence of Aliens and the Right of Asylum), they are considered to commit an illegal entry. the operational criteria for the characterization of illegal entry is the description of circumstances: the regular or irregular entry determinates the final category. However, from a migratory perspective the operational criteria would be the "wish to establish himself" and not the "regularity" or "irregularity" of his/her entry and stay. These legal categories deal with an expression of public interest in which the individual is the object of the legal category and not the origin. The paradox lays on keeping the "solidarity crime" where the decriminalization of illegal stay

The fact that only the enumerated categories of migrants are eligible to legal residence (temporarily or not) provides us with an initial element of attachment to a specific territory. This results in a reproduction of a strictly national scheme closely linked to national identity. If national legislation codifies categories of migrants eligible to stay legally, the State will always perceive migration as an exteriority. That is why detention measures have become the rule within national contexts, by systematizing the detention of migrants in an irregular situation without giving an individualized cause. On the other hand, the EU Return Directive defines detention only as a measure of last resort, outlining that migration is not a crime per se, which has also been confirmed by the CJEU[6]. The systematization of detention operates both for asylum seekers and illegal third-country nationals, for asylum seekers in the respective refugee camps, and also the imprisonment of illegal third country nationals (because illegal entry is an offence within the French legal framework)[7]. At this point, we need to highlight that under international human rights law and under European law, detention of migrants and asylum seekers should be used only as a measure of last resort[8]. This is justified by the fact that detention of migrants and asylum seekers does not have a punitive purpose, but illegal entry constitutes an administrative offense. In countries like France the offense of illegal residence has been abrogated, but illegal entry is still penalised with a sentence of one year's imprisonment and a fine according to Article L. 621-2 of the Code on Entry and Residence of Foreign Nationals and the Right to Asylum (Ceseda Code)[9].

Furthermore, the proliferation of coercion within the EU, at the expense of the protection of fundamental rights of migrants, is an element that fortifies national sovereign decisions through extended and coercive detention of migrants and asylum seekers. In addition to that, in July 2015 the European

---

introduced by the regulation of 31 December 2012 could have been the occasion in order to abrogate easily the article L. 622-1 of the Ceseda or at least its component relative to the facilitation to illegal stay.

6 See Return Directive, Directive 2008/115/EC of the European Parliament and of the Council of 16 December 2008 on common standards and procedures in the Member States for returning illegally staying third-country nationals. See also See Judgment of the Court 7 June 2016, Sélina Affum contre Préfet du Pas-de-Calais et Procureur général de la cour d'appel de Douai, Affaire C-47/15, ECLI:EU:C:2016:408.

7 National French legislation codifies the illegal entry as an offense liable to a sentence of one year's imprisonment and a fine (article L.621-2 French Ceseda).

8 See Judgment of the Court 7 June 2016, Sélina Affum contre Préfet du Pas-de-Calais et Procureur général de la cour d'appel de Douai, Affaire C-47/15, ECLI:EU:C:2016:408.

9 See Article L. 621-2 of the Code on the Entry and Stay of Foreign Nationals and the Right of Asylum (Ceseda Code): "A foreign national who is not a national of a Member State of the European Union shall be liable to a sentence of one year's imprisonment and a fine of EUR 3 750: 1. if he has entered the territory of Metropolitan France without satisfying the conditions referred to in Article 5(1)(a), (b) and (c) of [the Schengen Borders Code] and without having been admitted to that territory pursuant to Article 5(4)(a) and (c) of that [code]; the same shall apply where an alert has been issued for the purpose of refusing the foreign national entry pursuant to an enforceable decision adopted by another State party to the [CISA]; 2. or if, arriving directly from the territory of a State party to [the CISA], he has entered the territory of Metropolitan France without complying with the requirements of Article 19(1) or (2), Article 20(1) and Article 21(1) or (2) thereof, with the exception of the conditions referred to in Article 5(1)(e) of [the Schengen Borders Code] and in Article 5(1)(d) where the alert for the purpose of refusing entry does not result from an enforceable decision adopted by another State party to the [CISA];".

Commission, through one of its members, stressed the fact that detention should not be ended prematurely because it consists of an important tool for efficient migration control and management. In December 2015, the European Council President confirmed the previous statement of the European Commissioner for Migration and Home Affairs by claiming it to be necessary to have detention periods of up to 18 months for asylum-seeker screening proceedings. 18 months is the maximum length of detention permissible under the EU Return Directive[10]. The question to answer remains the same: during this extended period of maximum 18 months of detention, are fundamental rights of migrants and asylum seekers efficiently protected? What is the status of migrants and asylum seekers within detention facilities?

The relative jurisprudence of the European Court of Human Rights has revealed in the affair M.S.S. v. Belgium that the extreme material poverty when it comes to detention facilities can be considered as degrading and inhuman treatment based on "*official indifference [of a state administration] when in a situation of serious deprivation or want incompatible with human dignity*". In this case, unsafe living conditions regulated by a Member State are qualified as violations of article 3[11] of the ECHR. Similarly, in the N.S. v. Secretary of State for the Home Department, the ECHR judged that the conditions were inadequate for the reception of asylum seekers and "*applicants are either detained in inadequate conditions or they live outside in destitution, without shelter or food*". Once again, this treatment is qualified as inhuman or degrading under Article 4 of the Charter[12] . This leads us to interrogate the actual meaning of "degrading and inhuman treatment" when it comes to camps of asylum seekers. For this specific case, the extended detention of asylum seekers within camps is also accompanied by a lack of many fundamental rights such as: access to basic sanitation and medical care, subjection to extreme violence at the hands of security forces or intra-camps. The systematization of detention practices is already a factor of deprivation of fundamental rights of migrants that comes to be added to the relativization of the meaning of "inhuman and degrading treatment". At the same time, systemic deficiencies of Member States[13], like in the M.S.S. v. Belgium and Greece affair, are not being seriously taken into account. Whereas other Member States without systemic deficiencies are not willing to take over, considering the former ones to be in breach of their international obligations to protect displaced persons from inhuman and degrading treatment. This should also be

---

10 See Return Directive 2008/115 EU, op. cit.

11 See M.S.S. v. Belgium and Greece, App. No. 30696/09 Eur. Ct. H.R., (2011) (citing Budina v. Russia, Dec. No. 45603/05 (2009)).

12 See Judgment of the Court (Grand Chamber) of 21 December 2011, N. S. (C-411/10) v Secretary of State for the Home Department.

13 Systemic deficiency of a Member State can be the inherent difficulty of the State to manage a specific domain of its exclusive competence. Article 29 of the Schengen Borders Code can be invoked in cases of serious deficiencies in the carrying out of external border controls which in themselves constitute a serious threat to public policy or internal security. On this topic see Peers S. (2015, December 2). Can Schengen be suspended because of Greece? Should it be? [Blog post]. Retrieved from http://eulawanalysis.blogspot.com/2015/12/can-schengen-be-suspended-because-of.html

stressed as a criticism of the Dublin Regulation, and as a general reflexion on EU Regulation 610/2013 that guarantees, *"decisions under this Regulation shall be taken on an individual basis"*, where Member States should act in accordance with protections of fundamental rights and the principle of *non-refoulement*[14].

Habermas argues that the only source of legitimacy is the democratic procedure from which law is generated and produced. However, the democratic procedure is conceived as a *"method that creates legitimacy out of legality"* (Habermas, 2004). This rationalization of the democratic procedure has an impact on fundamental rights because it alters the meaning of the universality of fundamental rights which is *"no longer essential but becomes communicational"* (Chabot, 2006). In this sense, the democratic praxis tends to introduce a certain relativism of values that need to be subject to a democratic choice (*idem*). This certain relativism of values has resulted a reversed set up of the relationship between democracy and human rights: human rights establish democracy and not the other way round. Otherwise, democracy would become negotiable. This rationalization of fundamental rights can be found in all relative policies relevant to migration and asylum as demonstrated in the above example of systematization of detention practices based on a rational control and management of migration flow.

Soft Law and National Unilateral Decisions

The second element of our main hypothesis is that soft law results from the transition of the model of national and inter-governmental governance to a model of European governance. Traditionally, migration flow control was administrated by a guards employed by states, embodying a traditional concept of the State protecting its sovereignty at its borders. Later on, international agreements regulated migration flow through a migration control at an international level[15]. And today, we have the EU with its agencies, FRONTEX and operation Sophia[16] cooperating with NGO's managing the situation of incontrollable migration flow. This transforms migration control into migration management with the involvement of various actors at the core of Member States. Thus what might have been seen before as a violation of national sovereignty is now considered to be a matter of cooperation between individual Member States and the EU. Nevertheless, many States such as Austria and Germany are not willing to accept this migration flow management. They

---

14 Regulation (EU) 610/2013 art. 1, § 3, O.J. (L 182).

15 For example see the reaction of international actors regarding the EU-Turkey Statement, Amnesty International: EU's Reckless Refugee Returns to Turkey, (2016, June 3). Retrieved from https://www.amnesty.org/en/latest/news/2016/06/eus-reckless-refugee-returns-to-turkey-illegal/ ;
Human Rights Watch: EU: Turkey Mass-Return Deal Threatens Rights, (2016, March 15). Retrieved from https://www.hrw.org/news/2016/03/15/eu-turkey-mass-return-deal-threatens-rights.

16 The mandate of Operation Sophia includes several tasks that could endanger migrants' fundamental rights, It stills remains a question without answer how the mission of operation Sophia will be operationalised in accordance with the international legal principle of non-intervention (Article 2(4) UN Charter. See more on the ambiguity of compatibility of Operation Sophia with fundamental rights : Wauters E. and Cogolati S. (2016), retrieved from https://www.law.kuleuven.be/iir/nl/onderzoek/working-papers/wp180wauters-cogolati.pdf.

derogate from the Schengen Borders Code (SBC) and they reintroduced the Schengen borders police control[17]. The Schengen area implies the disappearance of internal borders, yet the migratory crisis and terrorism have given grounds to certain States to re-establish these borders. This is permitted for matters related to public order or internal security by the European legislation under Article 23 of the SBC. However, this has not been the case, and may appear to represent a turn back towards the exercise of national sovereignty and negation of EU law? Italian authorities, for example, issued temporary residence permits for humanitarian reasons when processing undocumented North African immigrants coming from Tunisia, who arrived on their national territory before 5 April 2011. These residence permits granted them an automatic right to move freely within the Schengen area. Some EU Member States expressed concerns about the Italian residence permits and France reintroduced checks at its border with Italy[18]. That also shows that only the frontline countries are the one affected by the "refugee crisis", so concepts like protection of public order, the fight against "abusive" free movement or against "social tourism" reappear in order to exclude immigrants from the other Member States. There was actually a proposition (Dutch proposal) of the creation of a mini-Schengen area to exclude States unable to manage migratory flows, or even the construction of walls within Europe itself (Benedicto and Brunet, 2018). In this way we can ask whether EU external borders have become pathways that in effect promote the immigration of desirable third country nationals. These migrants often contribute to their host countries by stimulating economic output, scientific research, and cultural development. There is also the humanitarian element of family reunification and offering protection to refugees that results. We see this, for example, in the conditions under which residence permits are issued under French law. Here residency

---

17 Council Decision implementing decision (EU) 2016/894 of 12 May 2016 setting out a recommendation for temporary internal border control in exceptional circumstances putting the overall functioning of the Schengen area at risk. See also Commission Opinion of 23.10.2015 on the necessity and proportionality of the controls at internal borders reintroduced by Germany and Austria pursuant to Article 24(4) of Regulation No 562/2006 (Schengen Borders Code), C(2015) 7100 final.

18 See the report of the parliamentary assembly of the Council of Europe, The arrival of mixed migratory flows to Italian coastal areas Report, Committee on Migration, Refugees and Displaced Persons Rapporteur: Mr Christopher Chope, United Kingdom, EDG, Section 3.3 of the Report entitled Return Policies states : "On 5 April 2011, Italy reached an agreement with Tunisia following which Italy granted a six months temporary residence permit to most of the Tunisian migrants who arrived in Italy between 1 January and 6 April 2011 in exchange for strengthened border controls with a view to preventing departures by Tunisia. As a consequence, irregular departures from Tunisia declined significantly. Approximately 18 000 humanitarian permits were issued by the Italian authorities. These were extended on request in October 2011 for about 5 000 Tunisians and again automatically in May 2012." See also Section 3.4 of the same report, entitled Informal way out of the country which states : "[...] irregular migrants may unofficially be encouraged to go up North and cross over the Italian border into other Schengen countries. This was obvious in the case of the Tunisians in 2011. Many of them drifted into irregularity and moved on to other European countries, as the permits granted by Italy allowed for travel within the Schengen zone. [...] The ease with which irregular migrants can find a way out of Italy and drift north into the rest of Europe is an issue which other European countries have criticised Italy about and is one which will need to be tackled. It was particularly obvious in the case of Tunisians in 2011, and it will continue to be a bone of contention until dealt with". Retrieved from http://assembly.coe.int

rules are barriers that prevent undesirable third-country nationals from entering the territory of EU Member States (Basilien-Gainche, 2015).

This retreat of several Member States is affirmed by the emergence of unilateralism and bilateralism. This means that either Member States can decide unilaterally to derogate from the SBC, as we mentioned above, or through bilateral agreements with third states in order to control migration flow without being bound to EU measures[19]. On the one hand, there is the example of the bilateral agreement of Italy with Libya, Niger and Morocco. On the other hand, unilateral sovereign decisions from Member States include different approaches from the Member States and could lead to a retreat from EU law. National solutions have been adopted, sometimes extra-protectionist, in order to limit the reception of asylum-seekers from Member States such as Hungary and Czech Republic (Grigonis, 2016). In the specific case of Hungary, a wall was built on its borders, and the Hungarian State has created an agreement with Serbia that demands that all asylum applicants who cross the border from Serbia shall be automatically denied entry and shall be sent back to Serbia. In the case of the Czech Republic, the State declared there would be a permanent, on-going violation of asylum seekers' fundamental rights, such as the systematization and extension of detention practices, omission to provide information for free legal aid, strip-searching and confiscation of money for the mandatory payment per day of their involuntary stay in the detention centres. These voluntary violations of fundamental rights raise a more crucial question about the actual democratic character of Europe. In addition to that, Spain had built a series of fence systems in 2005 in their North African enclaves for people trying to climb over the barriers from the Moroccan side. These caused "unnecessary physical dangers" that should be avoided according to the UN's General Provision 2 of the Basic principles on the use of force and firearms by law enforcement officials. All the above measures implicitly demonstrate a violation of the principle of *non refoulement* and national solutions not attending to migrants' fundamental rights.

All the above national unilateral decisions result from the problem of migration management which is accompanied by an extended use of soft law. The extended use of soft law towards migration as a new mode of governance instead of hard law lowers 'sovereignty costs'. "*As soft instruments are not legally binding as such, they entail a smaller loss of autonomy for the cooperating (member) states than hard legal acts. Thus soft law offers a compromise between sovereignty-autonomy and order*" (Peters, 2011). It is worth asking the question if soft law is the most suitable solution for European migration policies. Especially when the externalized migration policy keeps populations in places, where they cannot

---

19 See the Commission Opinion of 23.10.2015 on the necessity and proportionality of the controls at internal borders reintroduced by Germany and Austria pursuant to Article 24(4) of Regulation No 562/2006 (Schengen Borders Code), C(2015) 7100 final. See also the Council Decision implementing decision (EU) 2016/894 of 12 May 2016 setting out a recommendation for temporary internal border control in exceptional circumstances putting the overall functioning of the Schengen area at risk.

trigger the EU or the Member States' jurisdiction[20]. Even if European policies do not qualify migration as a crime per se, they externalize migration outside the scope of EU law, transforming migration control to migration management. In that sense, one might consider this to be more a crisis of European policies rather than a migration crisis.

If human rights are considered to be universal, a permanent tension will not cease to reappear when it comes to talk about migration. If in today's Europe, human rights have become a battlefield between sovereignty claims to control borders and migrants' claims to access to a territory, we cannot help but question how can fundamental rights overcome this tension. If, as a result of sovereignty claims, human rights determine only the authorized or eligibility to legal residence of third-country-nationals, their legal content becomes less neutral and universal, or an "attempt by states to empty the categories of all human rights' content so that the *"illegal', [is the one] as defined and designated by their authorities"* (Costello, 2016).

Camps and Denationalization

The third element of our hypothesis would be the definition of "Hotspot" or "camp" neither of which is are legal terms. That means that until recently we did not have a legal instrument that determined the status of asylum seekers within the camps. Is there a legal vacuum within camps? Is the migrant living inside the camp a subject of law? Do we see camps as a temporary suspension of normality? In terms of law, camps should be the exception because there is no clear definition of their status, so no clear application of fundamental rights. Are we talking about a suspension or rights or an exception that actually becomes permanent? If the suspension of fundamental rights within camps becomes the rule, then the derogation from fundamental rights is institutionalized. It becomes the normality where it should be the exception.

The inquiries above are part of the denationalization process that includes policies implemented by non-state actors where private enterprises are involved in detention and the development of hi-tech mechanisms of databases collecting migrants' footprints (Bosworth, 2014). However, the intervention of these actors at a state level with the construction of camps of illegal migrants/asylum seekers at the territory of a Member State raises questions of effectiveness of fundamental rights. This takes into consideration that detention camps administrated by humanitarian actors do not have a clear legal status. In that sense, how can fundamental rights be guaranteed if there is a "legal vacuum" within the detention camps? Camps for migrants have not yet a legal determined status and they are used as an alternative to prison, which render individuals into a space of non-law, because they no longer are subjects of law. In this way, we see a camp as a heterotopy, a space of non-law (Foucault,

---

20 The example of the EU-Turkey Statement of 18 March 2016 is an agreement between the EU and Turkey relative to the rapid return of all migrants not in need of international protection crossing from Turkey into Greece and the take back of all irregular migrants intercepted in Turkish waters. See also Ziebritzki C. and Nestler R. (2018).

1967)[21]. We need to clarify that the UNCHR is governing administratively the camps, but these camps are still operating at the national legal order. So, if someone is responsible for the effectiveness of fundamental rights within camps, this is still the State. That means that even if we have passed from the traditional model of government to the model of European governance, the State is still responsible in matters of fundamental rights. But what happens when the State has a systemic failure? Here, the concept of governance is actually in retreat leaving all responsibilities to the State, something which is also confirmed by the extended use of soft law: agreements replace laws. This means that private actors gain a share in public power, yet without being integrated into the framework of legitimation and accountability that the constitution establishes for public actors. That leads us once more to the question of effectiveness of fundamental rights when migration policies are not directly administered by a public authority. Keeping in mind that public authorities are obliged to follow some structural methods of respect of fundamental rights. By this point of view, this is a weakening of the effectiveness of fundamental rights in terms of migration.

Sovereign rights were given up voluntarily because the states expected something in return: an increase in problem-solving capacity in matters that could no longer be effectively handled on the national level. In addition, the States usually retain a share in the decision-making process of the international institutions that now exercise these rights. But this cannot compensate for the decrease in constitutional legitimation and limitation of public power. The potential restraints of State power implies a loss in terms of effectiveness of fundamental rights. According to the German jurist Dieter Grimm

an internal erosion that started almost unnoticed in the wake of a transformation of statehood, domestically as well as internationally, and eventually cost the state the monopoly of public power over its territory. Today, the state shares its power with a number of non-state actors, most of them international organisations to whom sovereign rights have been transferred and whose exercise escapes the arrangements of national constitutions[22]" (Grimm, 2010).

According to Grimm, the internal erosion could endanger the capacity of the constitution to fulfil its claim of establishing and regulating all public power that has an impact on the territory where the constitution is in force (*idem*). Until now, public power of the state was without an external competitor within the territory, whereas now the state is unable to shield its borders from acts of a foreign public power. The raising question here is how the State can secure the comprehensive functioning of its constitution and leave no space for a lawless zone. And the specific question should be answered via the example of hotspots.

Dieter Grimm argues that public power does not mean State power anymore, because "public" can also be an international organisation. So, State power cannot be assimilated to public power anymore and this creates a

---

21 See also Foucault M. (2009) amd Basilien-Gainche M.-L. (2013).
22 See also Grimm (2005).

problem to the democratic legitimation. He argues that from a national legal point of view,

the constitution still emanates from the people but it can no longer secure that any public power taking effect within the state finds its source with the people and is democratically legitimized by the people. In sum, the emergence of an international public power does not render the constitution obsolete of ineffective. But to the extent that statehood is eroding, the constitution is in decline. It shrinks in importance since it can no longer fulfil its claim to legitimize and regulate all public authority that is effective within its realm (idem).

That means that if the highest normative instrument of fundamental rights is in decline –this is the Constitution-, how can fundamental rights become effective within a national legal order? Or, in other words, the transition from the model of government to the model of European governance should also be followed by a global mechanism of protection of fundamental rights. This cannot be achieved for the moment because the power of the EU is by no means unregulated but only embedded in a "closely-meshed net of legal norms". This confirms the lack of a democratic origin of the EU regulatory power because the EU does not decide upon its own legal foundation but receives this foundation by an agreement between its Member States. That results in two points that demonstrate a new reflection on the status of hotspots and fundamental rights: the first point consists of EU Treaties that do not enjoy democratic legitimacy that characterizes a constitution. Consequently, they cannot guarantee efficient, superior fundamental rights' protection at the level of the Constitution. The second point refers to the acts of public authority that do not emanate from the state and are not submitted to the requirements of the state's constitution. This affects their validity on the state's territory which does not depend on their being in harmony with the domestic constitution.

Externalization of European Borders

Regional agreements, bilateral agreements, IMO recommendations, EU directives, global agreements, the New York Declaration, are all instruments of protection of fundamental rights of migrants. They have been developed to deal with the migration challenge, and Europe has been being one of the main migration destinations. However, we attest a relativization of the area of freedom security and justice based on national penalization practices of detention for illegal entry[23]. This relativization is an additional element of the model of European governance that questions the effectiveness of fundamental rights. This is because current migration flow management, as part of the European model of governance, works with the externalization of EU borders towards third countries (as an example, see the EU-Turkey Statement). Initially the intention was to accommodate these persons in specific temporary structures, during the time their asylum application would be assessed.

---

[23] See more on the concept of crimmigration, Van der Woude M. and Van der Leun J. (2017).

However, some of these facilities have in effect become centres of detention, in which some analysts see deliberate violation of fundamental human rights. The 1951 Geneva Convention relating to the Status of Refugees, for example, lays down in Articles 32 and 33 a prohibition against the expulsion of asylum seekers from the frontiers *"of the territories where his life or freedom would be threatened"* and Turkey does not give a lot of proof of a safe third country. The result of this Statement are the devastating effects on the fundamental rights, such as derogations from the principle of *non-refoulement* and from the prohibition of collective expulsion. Nevertheless, the European Convention of Human Rights prohibits inhuman and degrading treatment[24], as well as the deprivation of personal liberty of migrants[25]. So, if there is no European jurisdiction for asylum seekers, we do not only have an externalization of borders but also an externalization of EU law. If refugee camps are hosted in third countries which are not safe, questions can be raised about the effectiveness of the application of fundamental norms of human rights. Excluded people are not merely to be excluded from European territory but also from European law (Spijkerboer, 2017). Do fundamental rights become a relative concept within this model of governance?

In order to analyse this assertion more, we need to clarify that the efforts within the EU for the externalization of borders is more than crucial. The judgment of the ECHR in the case J.R. and others vs. Greece is the first one that deals with the implementation of the EU-Turkey Statement and the « given legitimacy » to hotspots. The three Afghan nationals, who were arrested and placed in the 'Vial hotspot' of Chios, one day after the entry into force of the EU-Turkey Statement, applied for asylum and claimed that there was insufficient food, a lack of hygiene, the water supply had been often cut off, and medical care and legal assistance were scarce at the Vial hotspot. The applicants complained about the lack of information concerning the reasons of their detention, and the conditions and length of their detention. The Court pronounced that there has been no violation of article 5(1) of the ECHR as their detention had not been arbitrary and could not be regarded as "unlawful" within the meaning of Article 5(1). However, the Court pronounced a violation of article 5(2) because there was no adequate information leaflet that could provide them with sufficient details and possible remedies available. We must clarify that the above judgment did not rule on the legitimacy or the legal nature of the EU-Turkey statement. However, it related only to the violation of the Convention in this specific case. Nor did it address the question of whether Turkey qualifies as a 'safe third country' under Article 38 of the <u>Asylum Common Procedures Directive</u>[26].

---

24 Article 3 of the European Convention on Human Rights states : "No one shall be subjected to torture or to inhuman or degrading treatment or punishment".

25 Article 5§1 of the European Convention on Human Rights states : "Everyone has the right to liberty and security of person. No one shall be deprived of his liberty save in the following cases and in accordance with a procedure prescribed by law […]".

26 Common Procedures Directive, Directive 2013/32/EU of the European Parliament and of the Council

Conclusion

The arguments presented above point to a softening of a legal order potentially being a sign of the weakness of its normative power. This means relativism of values and inefficiency of fundamental rights. This emergence of soft law contrasts to the strong sovereign decisions to systematize detention within national legal orders This appears to confirm a resurgence of national patterns such as sovereignty, national governance models which were supposed to be set aside in favour of European multilevel governance. However, national courts (especially the Karlsruhe Court) are reluctant to conform to this idea. The Karlsruhe Court's decision of 30 June 2009 specifies that democratic legitimation exists only on a national level. They said that this is demonstrated by the way national decisions concerning migration policies are often much more powerful, often resulting in a high degree of detention practices for security reasons. So, the democratic legitimation of European governance in the specific field of migration becomes problematic when the softening of the European legal order works against the effectiveness of fundamental rights and cannot be achieved through soft law.

A relative effectiveness of fundamental rights within the national contexts can confirm the emergence of a relativism of values. The inter-subjectivity of rights, which until now was essential, becomes communicational in order to achieve a high level of democratic procedural rationality[27]. This relativization of fundamental rights through soft law increases the inherent contradiction of a plural European identity under construction (or perhaps more properly deconstruction). The challenge of European governance is how to transform the valorization of the procedural rationality to one of an essential nature, and thus lead democratic praxis to re-appropriate its origin. Nevertheless, this concept of procedural rationality establishes soft law as the fastest and most flexible solution to the migration challenge. The challenge is actually based on the re-appropriation of normative integrity and functional capacity of law during this transition to governance.

That leads us to ask the question about whether migration flow will always be a State matter. Whereas EU migration policies move from migration control to migration management, national migration policies move to an anti-migration national policy of " policing populations". Migration crisis is the can be seen a manifestation of a European identity crisis. As Jean Marc Ferry outlines, we have to deal with a triple crisis which includes a *telos' (finality)* crisis, an ethical crisis of political co-responsibility and a historical crisis of legitimation of the European project. In a national context, we see all types of legitimate

---

of 26 June 2013 on common procedures for granting and withdrawing international protection.

27 Jürgen Habermas' communicational rationality is oriented towards mutual conflict resolution through compromise (in contrast to strategic action). See on this topic Niemi J. I. (2005). See also Feteris E.T. (1999). According to the Stanford Encyclopedia of Philosophy "Communicative action is thus an inherently consensual form of social coordination in which actors "mobilize the potential for rationality" given with ordinary language and its telos of rationally motivated agreement ". Retrieved from https://plato.stanford.edu/entries/habermas/#TheComAct.

coercion such as the criminalization of illegal migrant, detention measures, reintroduction of Schengen controls. Whereas in the European context we see legitimate coordination and cooperation and multilevel governance. However, the extended use of soft law regarding migration constitutes the opposite of strong sovereign national decisions being taken based on criminal codes and criminal procedures. If national criminal codes are applied with an extensive use of detention or imprisonment of migrants, illegal entry across an internal border will continue to represent a crime merely on this sole ground. The systematization of detention measures is closely linked to the question of the effectiveness of fundamental rights within the European context. The relativization of fundamental rights goes along with the relativization in the areas of freedom, security and justice through the extensive use of soft law, which increases the inherent contradiction of the plural identity under (de-) construction.

In particular, this is the case when vulnerable people are not merely excluded from European territory, but also from European law (Spijkerboer, 2017). However, it seems that there is a quasi-ontological relationship between EU and migration, mainly because the concepts of free movement of people and the abolition of intra-European borders are constitutive elements of the European project. Finally, if the democratic legitimation within the EU has not yet succeeded, how can we evaluate the communicational procedural rationality of fundamental rights? The challenge is currently based on the re-appropriation of normative integrity and functional capacity of law (Kjaer, 2017) during this transition to new forms of governance.

References
Books and Journals

Basilien-Gainche M.-L. (2015). La norme et l'exception. L'effectivité en péril du droit d'asile en Europe. Annuaire du droit de l'Union européenne 2013, pp. 3-31.
Basilien-Gainche M.-L. (2015). The EU External Edges: Borders as Walls or Ways?. Journal of Territorial and Maritime Studies, North Asian History Foundation, 2 (1), pp. 97 – 117.
Basilien-Gainche M.-L. (2013). Etat de droit et états d'exception, Paris: PUF.
Bosworth M. (2014). Inside Immigration Detention. Oxford: Oxford University Press.
Chabot J.-L. (2006). Figures de la médiation et lien social, Paris: L'Harmattan, pp. 143-159.
Costello C. (2016). The Human Rights of Migrants and Refugees in European Law, Oxford: Oxford University Press.
Feteris E.T. (1999). Habermas' Theory of Communicative Rationality. Fundamentals of Legal Argumentation. Argumentation Library, vol 1. Dordrecht: Springer.
Foucault M. (1967). Des espaces autres, Hétérotopies, Dits Ecrits, t. IV, texte no 360, (or Conférence au Cercle d'études architecturales, 14 mars 1967: Architecture, Mouvement, Continuité, no 5 (1984): 46-49).
Foucault M. (2009). Le corps utopique - Les hétérotopies, éds. Lignes.
Grigonis S. (2016). EU in the face of migrant crisis: Reasons for ineffective human rights protection. International Comparative Jurisprudence, Volume 2, Issue 2, pp. 93-98.
Grimm D. (2010). The achievement of constitutionalism and its prospects in a changed world.

In P. Dobner and M. Loughlin (ed.), The Twilight of Constitutionalism ?, Oxford : Oxford University Press. pp. 14-16.

Grimm D. (2005). The Constitution in the Process of Denationalization. Constellations, Vol.12, Issue.4, pp. 447-463.

Habermas J. (2004). Pluralisme et Morale. Esprit, No 306, pp. 5-28.

Joly M. (2007). The European Union and the people, Oxford: Oxford University Press.

Kjaer P. (2017). European crises of legally-constituted public power: From the 'law of corporatism' to the 'law of governance'. European Law Journal, Vol. 23, Issue 5, pp. 417-430.

Niemi J. I. (2005). Jürgen Habermas's Theory of Communicative Rationality: The Foundational Distinction Between Communicative and Strategic Action. Social Theory and Practice, Vol. 31, No. 4, pp. 513-532.

Peers S. (2015, December 2). Can Schengen be suspended because of Greece? Should it be? [Blog spot]. Retrieved from http://eulawanalysis.blogspot.com/2015/12/can-schengen-be-suspended-because-of.html

Peters A. (2011). Soft Law as a new mode of governance. In Diedrichs, Reineres, Wessels (Ed.), The Dynamics of change in EU governance, Studies in EU Reform and Enlargement. Germany: Edward Elgar, pp. 21-51.

Ruiz Benedicto A. and Brunet P. (2018). Building walls, Fear and securitization in the European Union, Centre Delàs d'Estudis per la Pau, Transnational Institute, Barcelona. Retrieved from https://www.tni.org/files/publication-downloads/building_walls_-_full_report_-_english.pdf

Spijkerboer T. (2017). Bifurcation of Mobility, Bifurcation of Law. Externalization of migration policy before the EU Court of Justice. Journal of Refugee Studies 31 (2018), pp. 216-239.

Wallis E. (2018, November 15). Building walls in Europe, InfoMigrants. Retrieved from https://www.infomigrants.net/en/post/13359/building-walls-in-europe

Wauters E.and Cogolati S. (2016). Crossing the Mediterranean sea : EU migration policies and human rights. Leuven Centre for global governance studies Working Paper No. 180. Retrieved from https://www.law.kuleuven.be/iir/nl/onderzoek/working-papers/wp180wauters-cogolati.pdf

Van der Woude M. and Van der Leun J. (2017). Crimmigration checks in the internal border areas of the EU: Finding the discretion that matters. European Journal of Criminology, Vol. 14(1), pp. 27–45.

Ziebritzki C. and Nestler R. (2018, June 22). Implementation of the EU-Turkey Statement: EU Hotspots and restriction of asylum seekers' freedom of movement [Blog post]. Retrieved from http://eumigrationlawblog.eu/implementation-of-the-eu-turkey-statement-eu-hotspots-and-restriction-of-asylum-seekers-freedom-of-movement/

International and EU Acts and Judgments

Amnesty International: EU's Reckless Refugee Returns to Turkey, (2016, June 3). Retrieved from https://www.amnesty.org/en/latest/news/2016/06/eus-reckless-refugee-returns-to-turkey-illegal/

Council Decision implementing decision (EU) 2016/894 of 12 May 2016 setting out a recommendation for temporary internal border control in exceptional circumstances putting the overall functioning of the Schengen area at risk.

Commission Opinion of 23.10.2015 on the necessity and proportionality of the controls at internal borders reintroduced by Germany and Austria pursuant to Article 24(4) of Regulation No 562/2006 (Schengen Borders Code), C(2015) 7100 final.

Human Rights Watch: EU: Turkey Mass-Return Deal Threatens Rights, (2016, March 15). Retrieved from https://www.hrw.org/news/2016/03/15/eu-turkey-mass-return-deal-threatens-rights

Judgment of the CJEU 7 June 2016, Sélina Affum versus Préfet du Pas-de-Calais et Procureur général de la cour d'appel de Douai, Affaire C-47/15, ECLI:EU:C:2016:408.

Judgment of the ECHR (2011), M.S.S. v. Belgium and Greece, App. No. 30696/09 Eur. Ct.

H.R.

Judgment of the CJEU (Grand Chamber) of 21 December 2011, N. S. (C-411/10) v Secretary of State for the Home Department.

Common Procedures Directive, Directive 2013/32/EU of the European Parliament and of the Council of 26 June 2013 on common procedures for granting and withdrawing international protection.

Return Directive, Directive 2008/115/EC of the European Parliament and of the Council of 16 December 2008 on common standards and procedures in the Member States for returning illegally staying third-country nationals.

Regulation (EU) 610/2013 art. 1, § 3, O.J. (L 182).

Report of the parliamentary assembly of the Council of Europe, The arrival of mixed migratory flows to Italian coastal areas Report: Committee on Migration, Refugees and Displaced Persons Rapporteur: Mr Christopher Chope, United Kingdom, EDG. Retrieved from http://assembly.coe.int